The Willow *(obscured)*
The Saga *(obscured)*

A sequel to the sequel to *The Wind in the Willows*

by

Kenneth Grahame

With additional reporting by

Emilia Ermine & Sally Stoat

Edited by David Bouchier

For Diane

The first listener to these tales

With much love

All the characters depicted in this book are real, and all the events really happened. Any resemblance to fictional characters living, not feeling well, or dead, is purely coincidental and should be ignored.

"There never was a true story

That could not be told better

In parables."

Edith Wharton

Dramatis Animalium

Mole – a fine fellow, but shortsighted.

Water Rat – another fine fellow, brave and ingenious.

Badger – more serious and sensible than most animals.

Otter and Little Portly – a family rarely out of the water.

Toad of Toad Hall – known (to himself) as The Great Toad.

Pegasus – a barge horse with political opinions.

The Messenger Mice – a dedicated troupe of field mice with a mission.

Dirty Rat 1 – a sly (and very dirty) motor mechanic.

Dirty Rat 2 – his brother, somewhat cleaner and not quite so clever.

Dirty Rat 3 – his other brother, an aeronautical rat.

The Laboratory Rats – much cleaner than the dirty rats.

Ms Tiggywinkle – motherly hedgehog with a distinguished ancestry.

Dennis – a dragon, rather smaller than the average.

Lord Slimy Toad – an imposter, eventually exposed.

The Beavers – a squad of practical hydrographers, always busy.

Edward Bear – an escapee from the Wide World.

Henrietta – a golden hamster, Edward's friend.

Various rabbits – more likely to play than to work.

Various squirrels – unlikely to do anything useful at all.

Various ducks – decorative but prone to gossip.

The Bank Bole – the most trusted banker on the Riverbank.

A vegetarian tiger – very polite and helpful.

Some crabs – rather crabby and unhelpful.

A seal – willing to give advice, but rather superior.

Agent Porky – a railway company representative (perhaps)

Sally Stoat and Emilia Ermine – the only reporter (at different seasons) for the *Riverbank Record.*

Some lawyers – usually foxes and weasels, never welcome.

Some female White Mice – who claim to be (and probably are) mistresses of the universe.

Hamish the Oracat – who claims to be (and is not) a Scottish wild cat and a prophet.

Oracula the Orakitten – a better prophet than the Oracat.

Willem the Old Goat – a traveler with unlikely tales to tell.

The Medical Bear – a skilled and generous fellow from the old zoo.

Mrs. Weasel and Wally – a family in (temporary) distress.

A Snake – discontented with his bad reputation.

An Eagle – a quick-thinking bird who saved Toad from his own folly.

Some helpful elephants, unhelpful alligators, and other former zoo animals.

Captain Ahab – a bold white duck.

A Dolphin – amused a being mistaken for a whale.

Intrusive Humans

Various policemen – only doing their duty.

The County Sheriff – a nasty piece of work.

The Chief Constable – an unforgiving bureaucrat.

A young film producer – disappointed by his epic.

A bargeman – happy to be over-compensated by Toad.

Developers and surveyors – unwanted and quickly ejected.

Some mysterious not-a-monks – better than most humans.

About the Author(s)

There is a charming mystery attached to this volume of *The Willows Chronicles,* which is confusingly dated 1908/2024.

There is every reason to suppose that the first tales of the Wild Wood and the Riverbank were collected as daily news by Emilia Ermine, also known as Sally Stoat, a reporter for *The Riverbank Record,* who was trying to compile a memoir for the famous Toad of Toad Hall, who was too lazy to write it himself.

Unfortunately, the memoir proved to be such a narcissistic and bombastic pack of lies that nobody would even consider publishing it. Mole, who had become friendly with Emilia after their midnight collision, offered to help by filling in the gaps with stories of other, more sensible animals along the Riverbank who Toad had ignored. When news of this project spread everyone wanted to know "Will I be in it?" and so of course everyone was in it. The result, as we all know, was *The Wind in the Willows,* a great success which was published in 1908 under the name of Kenneth Graham.

Emilia and Sally continued their reporting until communication was lost, for reasons that will be revealed but not explained later. They transformed

Toad's unsuccessful memoir into a full-scale history of the Riverbank community, and this is it.

This treasure trove of tales was rediscovered in 2023 and 2024. Nobody knows where it came from, but it is safe to say that the ghosts of ghostwriters Emilia and Sally have been hovering somewhere in the background. The rumor that their notes were edited more than a hundred years later by a superannuated English journalist with time on his hands has been dismissed by every animal who has been consulted, and by many who have not. The mystery remains.

Contents

One – the Return of Edward and Henrietta

Two – Badger is Thoughtful, Toad is Active

Three – A Hedgehog Emergency

Four – Toad Sets the World on Fire

Five – Making Willows History

Six – A Musical Interlude

Seven – The Mice Rearrange Everything

Eight – The First Spring

Nine – Headline News

Ten – Toad Has Two Secrets

Eleven – Conversation with a Bear

Twelve – The Wandering Weasel

Thirteen – The Accidental Astronaut

Fourteen – Amphibians on the Move

Fifteen – A Visit to the Monsters

Sixteen – Toad's Memoir

Seventeen – The Clock

Eighteen – After the Fall

Nineteen – The Unseen University

Twenty – The Return of Toad

Twenty-one – Dynasty

Twenty-two – A New World Symphony

Chapter one: The Return of Edward and Henrietta

Things were quiet in the Wild Wood, and all along the Riverbank, which was just the way the animals liked it. They still didn't understand the mysterious change that had come to their world, and this was a regular topic of speculation when they got together after dinner in the Hidden Cottage. But the speculation was eager rather than anxious. Life was better, and they wanted to find out why.

Badger had the chair this evening, as he usually did. Although he was now Badger Emeritus the animals still looked to him for leadership, guidance, and even for common sense – a rare commodity among these lively animals.

"I suppose we must assume that this change is permanent," he began, referring, as they all knew, to the strange wall that had separated them from the Wide World. It looked like mist, but nobody could walk through it, see through it, or fly over it, and nobody came through from the other side. The horse Pegasus, who had the most book learning, suggested that they call it by the dignified Latin name of *Limbus,* which means the border, but the more down-to-earth majority decided to call it simply The Wall.

The Oracat, who had descended from his mountain for this meeting, said: "If I believed in benevolent spirits, I would say that a benevolent spirit has done this to save us from the horrors of the Wide World. But I don't believe in spirits of any kind, so it must be some kind of physical or meteorological phenomenon previously unknown to science, or even to cats. Let's hope it has no more surprises in store for us. Cats don't like surprises."

The animals were impressed by the word "meteorological," but not by the rest of it, which sounded too much like one of the Oracat's typical pronouncements, an elaborate statement of the obvious.

"Well," said Badger firmly, "I think we can all agree that this Wall has been a good thing for us so far. We have had no disturbances from the Wide World – no cars, trains, airplanes, policemen, real estate developers, film makers or any of those annoying things that have plagued us for years. We can have a quiet life at last."

Toad, who hated the idea of a quiet life without roads or cars, wriggled uncomfortably in his seat but said nothing. But other animals were eager to contribute.

Water Rat had been much impressed by the almost magical power of maps during his sea adventure. A map was like a model or a painting of the real thing, he argued. Perhaps it could create the real thing, the way a recipe creates a pie. So, he proposed going back to Toad's library and consulting his untidy collection of maps to find a map of their territory, and what they could remember of the outside.

"What would we do next?" asked the Mole. But Rat had no answer to that.

Mole himself proposed some deep digging to burrow underneath The Wall, and Otter and not-so-little Portly suggested an underwater expedition for the same purpose. "But what if you got out and couldn't get back?" demanded Badger, and these plans were disapproved.

Ms Tiggywinkle the hedgehog was not sure about any of these schemes. Her philosophy was that everything that happened was a repetition of something that had happened before. But this was new, unless it was something old that had happened again, in which case it would un-happen eventually. She felt slightly confused, and left the thought unfinished. But she was sure that this was something beyond their experience, and they should not fight against it. After all, they were safe and happy, and their little world was a better place.

Pegasus the horse agreed. "Let's count our blessings," he said. "There's nothing outside in the Wide World that we want, so long as we have enough tuna for Hamish, and plenty of things out there that we don't want. So, I say, leave it alone." They were soon to discover that the nothingness "out there" beyond the wall was all too complete, and contained nothing that any sensible animal *could* want.

Sally Stoat, the second and only reporter from *the Riverbank Record,* was curled up in a corner dozing with her head on her notebook.

"Talk, talk talk. Aren't you all going to *do* anything?" she muttered. "This isn't much of a story."

Even with all this combined animal brain power, nobody could think of anything sensible to try that had not been tried already or rejected as silly or dangerous. Toad boasted that he would be able to crash through to the Wide World in a powerful motor car, but this was too violent to please the other animals. They already saw The Wall as something semi-sacred and not to be touched. Toad was silenced but continued to think about his exciting idea. There was no problem, in his opinion, that could not be solved by a powerful, speedy machine. There might still be roads on the outside, as there had been before, long straight roads with no speed limits and, perhaps, no policemen. Toad sank into an ecstatic dream.

In fact, there was no good reason to do anything. They had, as Ms Tiggywinkle had pointed out, everything they wanted and, as Badger had said, perfect peace. The farm animals who had found themselves within The Wall quickly forgot about being domesticated and joined the rest of the animal family. The horses and donkeys formed a small society of their own around Pegasus, and only the fish in the river didn't know or care what had happened. Food was abundant in their world. There was a whispered proposal to turn Toad's estates into a farm, although this had not been mentioned to Toad himself yet. A minor supply crisis over the Oracat's canned tuna was solved when it was revealed that Mole, following some heavy hints from the cat, had providentially laid in a huge supply in the storage room of his Bistro before the world's cat food factories vanished.

A silence fell on the chattering group, and they heard a timid knock at what would have been a door, if there had been a door. They all turned around and jumped up, even the somnolent reporter, because the utterly unexpected visitors were Edward Bear and his friend Henrietta the Golden Hamster.

"How did you get here?" they chorused, more or less all at once, and the two embarrassed and slightly bedraggled figures were brought into the center of the circle.

After rest and refreshment Edward felt better, and less embarrassed about his earlier precipitate departure from the Wild Wood. He and Henrietta were urged to tell their story because it had to be something remarkable. They began hesitantly, but with growing confidence, to explain how they had come from the chill nothingness outside, through the impenetrable Wall, into the warm somethingness of the Hidden Cottage.

Edward and Henrietta's Story

"It was the strangest thing," began Edward, who was a sturdy and sensible bear, not given to mystical fancies. "Everything was normal at home, Henrietta sat in her cage or ran on her wheel,"

"It was very boring" put in Henrietta.

"And I sat on the sofa and was carried up to the bedroom at night. Then a couple of weeks ago things became...irregular. Our people didn't come or go at the usual times, they forgot to switch lights off, or left them on all the time, and the whole house was sort of blurred and confused."

"They forgot to feed me," Henrietta said resentfully. "I had to go to the kitchen and feed myself. I must say the food was better in there."

"The house sort of faded away, the people disappeared completely, and my television stopped working." (Readers concerned about anachronism should note that this was not a real television, but an 8 mm hand-cranked silent film projector. "Television" was a word the clever bear had invented decades ahead of its time).

"It was all very quiet," added the Hamster. "There were no storms or explosions or anything. It was as if the world was going to sleep, but we were wide awake. In the end we found ourselves outside in a sort of flat, cloudy landscape. The garden was gone, and all the other houses were gone. We had to leave our friend Tardy the family tortoise, we couldn't find him," she concluded sadly.

"There were other creatures moving in different directions," Edward continued. "They seemed to be happy to be out of their houses and out in the world, and they seemed to know where they were going. We recognized some of them: That chump Winnie the Pooh and his funny friends, Paddington with his silly sou-wester and wellington boots, and lots of other bears. Some of them had even stopped for a picnic."

"It was a regular moving toyshop," squeaked Henrietta, rather disapprovingly, "But there were some real animals too - rabbits, cats and dogs, and so on – the usual domestic menagerie."

"I don't know what you mean by 'real animals' grumbled Edward.

"We seemed to know which way to go," Henrietta continued, ignoring this, "Almost as if there was a path, but it wasn't a path you could see. Eventually we came to this wall and stopped. We didn't know what to do. Edward was a brave bear (he did his best to look brave) and tried to put his arm through, and it went right through. So, we tried to walk through together, and we did. It was cold for a moment then there was warm sunshine again, and colors came back, and here we were quite close to the Wild Wood."

"I wanted to bring Henrietta to a safe place," Edward explained. "And this was the only safe place we knew."

Henrietta blushed a little, although it is difficult for a creature with red and gold fur to blush successfully.

"Of course, of course," said Mole, and she blushed again."

"What I want to know," said Water Rat, scratching his head in perplexity, "Is what actually *happened*.

"Yes," urged Sally Stoat, now fully alert and scribbling furiously in her notebook, "Tell us what actually happened so we can understand what it means and I can get a decent headline out of it. Nobody's going to read a story called **NOTHING HAPPENED IN THE WIDE WORLD."**

"That's the problem, you see," said Edward. "Nothing was exactly what did happen and we don't know how or why."

Some of the senior laboratory rats who felt that work in the kitchen was beneath them, had taken off their chef's hats and resumed their white coats, spectacles, and clipboards. The chief lab rat had a scientific theory to offer. He argued that the place they had called the Wide World had been an unsuccessful experiment, a problem that often happened in scientific studies. The human creatures who populated and overpopulated the Wide World had been a disappointment – violent, predatory, cruel to animals, destructive to the planet, and not half as clever as they thought they were. The mysterious all-powerful controllers of the experiment had simply deleted these annoying creatures and most of their works, leaving animals untouched. The Wild Wood was preserved as an interesting anomaly and a possible model for a better version of the Wide World.

"That's the logical, scientific explanation," concluded the Chief Lab Rat, with the smug air of an animal who has ended the discussion.

"It sounds like the beginning of a new religion to me," muttered Pegasus.

"But who are they?" asked the bewildered Mole. "Who are these mighty and powerful controllers that we can't see?"

"Not us Rats!" said the chief rat hastily. "We won't point a finger at any species but there's a rumor in the rodent science community that White Mice were responsible."

Nobody paid much attention to the messenger mice, who were squeaking in indignation. Badger came to their defense.

"We have no White Mice here," he reminded everyone. Our brave Messenger Mice are a tasteful gray, and the wood mice are brown."

Henrietta the Golden Hamster spoke up. "Some people in the Wide World had white mice as pets," she told them, "But they kept themselves to themselves, always running through mazes or solving complicated hidden cheese problems. They looked down on the rest of us, even though they were so small."

Few animals really believed the White Mice theory, although the messenger mice looked a little wistful. How could mice do all that? It was too ridiculous – and these were animals who, having known Toad, had plenty of experience of the ridiculous. But they liked the idea that these great powers, whoever they were, had spared the Wild Wood community and protected them with the white Wall. Some began secretly to think of themselves as the Chosen Animals.

Eventually, after a great deal of time and time wasting, the committee reached the decision that all good committees must reach: they decided to do nothing. This pleased everybody and they all adjourned to Mole's Bistro for a celebratory dinner.

Chapter two: Badger is Thoughtful, Toad is Active

Badger was thoughtful after this meeting but kept his thoughts to himself. He brushed aside the metaphysical questions and concentrated on The Wall itself, and how it might affect their little world.

Who or what can come in from outside, he wondered? Is there just one place like this, or are there many, and how can we know? Who had done this, and why? Is it a refuge or a trap? All these questions would be answered in due course, in the most surprising possible way.

But at this stage it was what Sherlock Holmes (some of whose stories Badger had in his collection) would have called a three-pipe problem, and unfortunately Badger didn't have even one pipe.

It was obvious that some animals could come through The Wall from outside, as Edward and Henrietta had done. But they hadn't seen many strangers, so perhaps only those with some connection to the Wild Wood could return to it. This theory was confirmed the very next day when Mole, hurrying from his home at Mole End to the Hidden Cottage, tripped over what seemed to be a rock that hadn't been there before and fell flat on his face.

"Do watch where you're going," said the rock in a gruff voice, and Mole saw that it had a small, wizened head with indignant black eyes.

"You must be a tortoise!" said Mole in astonishment.

"And you must be a Mole," said the tortoise. "I always heard that moles were shortsighted."

After this unpromising start the tortoise became more friendly. His name was Tardy, he said, and he had lived in the same house as Edward Bear and Henrietta Hamster, until the house vanished. "When they started walking, I couldn't keep up," complained Tardy, "And I've only just arrived here. Is this the right place?"

"It is, it is," cried Mole happily. "Your friends are safe in the Hidden Cottage, and I'm going there now. Come along."

Tardy came along, but so slowly that Mole was late for the breakfast service at his Bistro.

It was a happy reunion once the initial misunderstanding had been sorted out.

"We thought you were lost in the garden," Henrietta explained contritely. "We looked and looked and called and called."

"We thought you had vanished with everything else," said Edward, "So we started walking. There seemed to be nothing else to do. But here you are, so everything's all right again."

Tardy grudgingly accepted their apologies and settled down to a late breakfast of lettuce leaves.

This arrival answered one of Badger's questions. It seemed that creatures with Wild Wood connections could pass through The Wall. But it left a great many mysteries, and Badger made a decision.

"We need information, we need facts," he declared. "There's no point in just dreaming things up. We need to investigate this Wall thoroughly, which means setting up an expedition."

Badger's eclectic library included part of a book about an expedition, which had impressed him. Two humans called Lewis and Clark had explored thousands of miles on an unknown continent, noting down and describing everything they saw. Surely it could not be too difficult to do the same with the much smaller territory around the Wild Wood and along the Riverbank? All they needed was for two intrepid explorers to volunteer.

When Badger explained this plan to a general meeting of the community he was met with an uncomfortable silence. Most animals had no notion of exploring more than a few yards from their homes. The point about unknown territory was that it was unknown, and the general opinion was that it should stay that way.

It was obvious to everybody, except Water Rat and Mole, that they should be the explorers, as two of the most senior and sensible animals. They reacted with alarm. Mole complained that he had never been sensible (many other animals agreed), and that in any case he was a shortsighted underground animal with a busy bistro to look after. The Water Rat announced that, far from being senior, he was quite young at heart and too irresponsible for a task like this. He just wanted to stay on the Riverbank with his painting and poetry.

These declarations started a long and disorderly discussion. The two intrepid stay-at-homes gradually yielded to the pressure of public opinion. Mole said he would go if they could carry a tent and enough food supplies for the trip, no matter how long it was. Ratty wanted to take along his painting equipment to record the journey. But how could they carry all that stuff? It seemed totally impractical until another voice joined in.

"What about the old caravan?" asked Pegasus, mildly. Nobody had noticed his head poking through the cottage window, but they turned to him at once. Pegasus had plenty of horse sense, and his reputation for wisdom stood almost as high as Badger's. Now he had solved their problem. The old caravan, which had already featured in two of their adventures, would allow the explorers to travel in comfort all around their world with any amount of food and equipment.

"They can only use the caravan if you agree to pull it," said Badger, pointing out the obvious.

Pegasus tried to look like a horse who was making a great sacrifice. In fact, he had been rather bored lately, with no long journeys to go on and Toad busy with one of his secret projects.

"Oh, I don't mind," he conceded, with just the right tone of reluctant self-sacrifice. And so, it was decided. The old caravan was hauled out of Toad's stables, the animals began cleaning it while Mole loaded enough food for a regiment of explorers and Water Rat collected paper and paints for both of them, and whatever reading material might be useful, including the (incomplete) saga of Lewis and Clark.

It was while looking through this book that Rat remembered his former enthusiasm for maps. When he had been almost blown out to sea during his sailing adventure, he had been rescued thanks to an old map from Toad's library which had led his friends to his landing place. A map was exactly what they needed so that they could record their journey and see what had changed. Toad let them take as many maps as they wanted. He was busy with what he considered a far more serious scheme.

It took time to get all this together. Ms Tiggywinkle agreed to look after Mole's Bistro with help from the Chef Rats, and one day the caravan set off, heavily loaded with food and yellowing maps. They had scarcely started when Ms Tiggywinkle called for them to stop.

"Wrong way," she called. "It's bad luck to go around the world Widdershins."

They had no idea what she meant, but obligingly turned around, crossed the bridge, headed clockwise towards Toad Hall, and were soon out of sight. All the stay-at-home animals cheered and went back to their breakfasts.

"Widdershins," muttered the horse, who had met a few gipsies in his time. "What superstitious nonsense." But, despite himself, he was just as happy to be going the lucky way.

Toad and his reluctant companion Slimena watched the expedition leave from one of the upper rooms in Toad Hall. The gaudy caravan moved slowly across the landscape in a more or less straight line, until it vanished into the haze.

"Good luck to them," thought Toad. "Just wait till they get back and see what *I* have accomplished." Slimena knew he was up to something. "If you want to go fast, just jump off the roof," she screeched. But he ignored her.

Toad had had only one idea from the beginning, and it was taking shape in the stables where the wreckage of Toad's old automobiles were stored. The dirty rats, who had somehow survived and multiplied without getting any cleaner, were at work on a project of bricolage to create one working car out of the remains of several others. Toad had specified that it must be both fast and heavy, and the rats had taken his words literally, as rats tend to do. It was nearing completion and looked like a cross between a racing car and a tank. Toad named it "The Destroyer."

He had determined from the start to crash through The Wall with a powerful machine and race along the empty roads that he imagined must be on the other side. By way of preparation, he had assembled a wardrobe for himself that combined elements of the racing driver, the wealthy connoisseur of motoring, and the hero of discovery. Toad wanted an audience for this triumph, so he chose a date and a place and spread the news far and wide throughout the Wild Wood and the Riverbank.

No animal or bird could resist this and, on the appointed day, a disorderly crowd assembled by a straight stretch of road leading up to the blank face of The Wall, not far from Toad Hall.

While this lunatic plan was going forward the more sensible animals were plodding around the perimeter of their world in the caravan, pulled by Pegasus. On the first evening they pulled up on a quiet field and Mole jumped into the caravan to make some tea. He opened the big brown teapot and heard a squeak of indignation from inside.

"Can't a fellow get any sleep around here," demanded a voice, and a small, furry face appeared, blinking in the light.

"We seem to have a stowaway," Mole called to the others.

"Stowaway, phooey," said the creature. "I live here, I'm a dormouse, and my name is Drowsy – no jokes please."

"Why were you sleeping in the teapot?" asked Water Rat who had come to see what the fuss was about.

"It's traditional, but it's not very comfortable, and people will keep on making tea," grumbled the dormouse. "It was very peaceful here until you fellows decided to go for a jaunt in the caravan."

They soothed the dormouse as best they could, and offered him a cup of tea, which he refused indignantly. He was a handsome creature but, once he was awake, rather too talkative, reciting poems and proposing riddles, as dormice usually do when they are awake.

The next day, having got little sleep themselves because of Drowsy's inane chatter, they resumed their exploration, trying to be systematic about it. Every hour or two they stopped while Water Rat hammered a small wooden stake into the ground right up against the edge of The Wall, and marked their position as best he could on the old map he had borrowed from Toad. It was soon obvious that the boundary was not, as they had imagined, a circle, but a wildly irregular line that zig-zagged this way and that. It avoided towns and villages but included some farms. When they got to the sea, where Rat had had such a disagreeable adventure, they found that the river still ran into it as before, the waves still splashed on the shore, and The Wall was way out to sea, like a cloud on the horizon. The little seaside town had vanished. It was all very puzzling.

At every stop, Rat and Mole got out their painting equipment, and spent some time capturing the scene while Pegasus sighed wearily and dozed. Rat placed his easel facing the mysterious Wall, and Mole faced the other way with his drawing pad.

A few days later they returned safely to the Riverbank with a complete map and no more idea of what it meant than they had had at the start. Despite all their careful observation they had found no gaps in the Wall, and no places where they could see over or through it.

Their artistic efforts had been only partially successful. Rat brought back a number of pictures that were white all over except for a small wooden stake painted at the bottom of each one, and Mole had a collection of riotous, brightly colored canvases that nobody could understand but everybody loved. Two of these classic examples of Mole Art even found their way onto the walls of Badger's distinguished home, and many more decorated the dining room of Bistro Mole.

The moment they returned excited rabbits gathered around the caravan to tell them that Toad was about to attempt something extraordinary, and perhaps very dangerous. Pegasus sighed some more, and Badger confirmed the bad news.

"The fool is going to try to drive through The Wall," he told them. "He has built a big, heavy car that he thinks will carry him to the other side. Goodness knows what he expects to find there."

The whole population gathered at the place Toad had chosen, a straight stretch of road behind Toad Hall that led up to the nearest part of The Wall. His monstrous, ugly Destroyer, pointed at one end like a battering ram, was pushed out onto the road by a team of Dirty Rats, and the engine started with a dull roar and a cloud of smoke. Toad appeared in his gaudy outfit, which included an iron hat with a spike on it from one of the suits of armor in the Hall and climbed aboard with great ceremony.

"Now you will see what Toad can do," he announced, waving grandly to the crowd of spectators, and without further ado he let in the clutch and went racing straight towards the blank, white Wall.

There was the sound of collective breath being held, and then the most peculiar gurgling, sucking sound as The Destroyer reached The Wall, went straight through, and vanished.

Toad was left sitting on the ground in front of the crowd of spectators, dazed and completely naked. All his elaborate clothing, including his iron hat, had followed the car, and Toad himself had been rejected.

The rabbits were laughing so hard that they couldn't speak, but everyone else had something to say.

"What did I tell you?" said the Oracat, who had not actually predicted anything remotely like this.

Badger said it was a disgrace. Water Rat said it was rather brave but not very sensible. Mole said it was embarrassing. The Dirty Rats said it was a shame to lose the Destroyer.

The Dormouse slept through it all.

Chapter three: A Hedgehog Emergency

Toad's latest exploit provided enough material for weeks of discussion and speculation along the Riverbank. The less serious animals thought it was the funniest thing they had ever seen and told it over and over. Those of a more thoughtful habit tried, without much success, to understand what it meant. One of the scientific rats pointed out the obvious: that an object could go through The Wall, but not a living thing, not even a toad. But this, like saying that the sky is up, was no explanation at all. Young rabbits and squirrels had been throwing stones through The Wall since it first appeared, then charging at it and bouncing off as if it was a trampoline – great fun until their mothers told them to stop for fear that one of them might go right through and vanish.

Slimena, who had watched the whole Destroyer fiasco from a room in Toad Hall, said that it simply demonstrated that Toad was as pig headed as any creature could be without actually being a pig. Toad himself stayed out of the argument. He suffered keenly from his public humiliation, and was depressed that he had not found his way back to the world of open roads and exhilarating speed. He felt confined, restricted, slowed down, in a way that other animals did not. Within a few days he had formed a new plan.

One day Mole found himself short-staffed in the Mole Bistro kitchen when none of the young hedgehogs – the Hoglets - turned up for work. Ms Tiggywinkle had sent all six of her offspring – now growing and sturdy youngsters – to help Mole in his busy restaurant to teach them the value of hard work and discipline. The Hoglets did not like this. None of their friends believed in hard work and discipline, especially the young rabbits who did nothing but eat and play.

But the Hoglets had become fairly reliable assistants, although somewhat given to fooling around and prickling the customers for fun, and Mole was worried when they failed to appear. He sent a messenger mouse to Ms Tiggywinkle, who soon appeared in person at the Bistro.

"They're not at home," she told Mole. "I can't find them in any of their usual places."

This was cause for a general alarm. Young animals could not just disappear. There was nowhere for them to go. Water Rat was informed, and sent messenger mice to Badger, and Pegasus. A search party was quickly organized. They started by following the perimeter beside The Wall, on the theory that the Hoglets may have tried to burrow through and become stuck. They found no little hedgehogs but something else very surprising. The Wall had moved outwards a few inches, as shown by the wooden stakes that Rat had placed all the way round. The space where it had moved looked perfectly normal, with rough grass and occasionally a hedge or small tree growing.

This was even more worrying than the vanished hedgehogs. If The Wall kept moving back they would be exposed to the Wide World again, and they had grown accustomed to being safe from its intrusions and dangers. But there was nothing they could do at the moment.

After a fruitless search they consulted the Oracat, as they should have done at the beginning.

"It's fairly obvious," said that facile feline, pausing for a moment in his meal. "The Hoglets grew up in the old castle before they all moved to Toad Hall. They played there when they were young, and it must be full of secret places. If they want to have fun, they will go to the Old Castle."

The Oracat was right, as he occasionally was. The Hoglets had gone to the castle to play Dungeons and Dragons, taking Dennis the small dragon along with them. They had plunged into the labyrinth of rooms and corridors under the castle and, when it was time to go to work at Bistro Mole, they found that they were completely lost. Dennis was no help. "I lived up in the tower," he grumbled, "Not down here. Dragons are not rabbits."

The Hoglets had found one corridor, not much more than a tunnel, that seemed longer than the others and followed it, hoping that it would lead them outdoors and squabbling among themselves about who was to blame for getting lost. The corridor went on and on, and their candles were burning down when the tunnel turned sharply upwards and led them into a sort of gray twilight. There was nothing they recognized, just a featureless flat landscape. When they turned around, they saw to their horror that they were on the other side of The Wall that nobody could cross. Their own world had vanished. When they looked for the tunnel entrance that had brought them here, that too had vanished.

Never had a family of young hedgehogs been quite as frightened as this. They would have clung to one another, but their spines made it difficult. Only Dennis the Dragon kept his head.

"Remember what Mr. Badger told us," he said. "Only those who belong there can go through The Wall from the outside. We belong in there, so let's see if we can simply walk in."

They formed a line and marched nervously up to The Wall and straight through it, coming face to face with the frustrated search party outside the castle. Explanations and accusations kept them busy until they got back to Toad Hall, where the unhappy Hoglets suffered another round of reproaches from their anxious mother and from Mole, whose morning meal service had been disrupted.

But these clouds of disapproval soon passed. Everyone was delighted that the Hoglets were safe, and eager to hear about what they had found on the "Other Side."

"It was nothing, really," said Harold the oldest Hoglet, "Literally nothing. No land, no sky, no sun, no plants or buildings or animals, just nothing." They were pressed for details but had little more to say. "You can't describe nothing," they repeated, with some exasperation. They had brought one thing back, not from the nothingness outside but from a niche in one of the castle's dungeons, where it might have lain for a long time. It was a roll of rough paper that, when it was carefully unfolded, seemed to be an ancient map, drawn in brown ink and now much faded.

Water Rat, who loved maps, seized it and saw that it showed a crude version of their own beloved Riverbank territory, with the Wild Wood much larger, more like a forest *(Ye forest of Eden)*, the castle clearly drawn *(Ye castle of Earl Toady),* and even the Oracat's hill marked *(Ye Mountain of Ye Fairly Wise Hermit).* "What did I tell you?" said the Oracat, almost excited.

Romantic soul that he was, Rat immediately decided that this must be a treasure map, just like the ones he had read about in old books from Badger's library. But where was the treasure? What was the treasure? The adventure of the Hoglets was forgotten as all the animals turned their minds (those who had minds capable of being turned away from eating) to this thrilling prospect of treasure trove.

Naturally they all imagined the treasure differently. Mole thought first of food, wondering what could be preserved for so long, and then of ancient recipes. Badger imagined a trove of fine, leather-bound books. The Rats began dreaming about medieval garbage, always said to be the finest. The rabbits couldn't think what they wanted, and so just kept bouncing up and down singing "Treasure, Treasure, Treasure," until they had to be suppressed.

Nobody thought of gold or silver until Toad heard the news. Nobody else along the Riverbank had any use for gold or silver, but Toad immediately assumed that a vast horde must have been buried close to the castle. A dim cross or blot on the map persuaded him that it must be directly underneath the present site of Toad Hall. He kept this discovery to himself and, late at night, started digging in the basement of the hall in a frenzy of cupidity, imagining himself rich beyond the dreams of Avarice, although he had no idea who Avarice was, or what his bank balance may have been.

Toad soon became thin from digging and weary from lack of sleep. Slimena thought he had gone mad. "We have No use for gold or silver even if you find it," she screeched.

"I'll create a market," said Toad, stubbornly. "Everybody will get a few coins and they will multiply by themselves, I've read about it, money breeds money. Then everything will have a price, and I will fix the price, then all the coins will come back to me.

That's how it worked it in the Wide World." Slimena went off to her tower to take aspirin.

Meanwhile all of the animals and some magpies had spread out across. The landscape. The map was not actually very helpful, being so creased and crumpled and stained that any choice was guesswork. So the rabbits and the squirrels dug holes everywhere, finding many things like old boots and bottles, but no treasure.

Ms Tiggywinkle had been too preoccupied with her delinquent Hoglets to pay any attention to the treasure map. But the following day she found Water Rat outside Toad Hall with the map spread out in front of him. "It's a treasure map," he explained. "Everyone is searching."

Ms Tiggywinkle studied the map thoughtfully. "It looks familiar," she said, and turned the sheet over. "Oh, it's one of my props, you'll find my name on the back." There, in small, neat letters, were the words: The Medieval Experience guided by Ms Tiggywinkle. The map was a relic of Ms Tiggywinkle's successful enterprise at the castle a couple of seasons ago, when she had put on guided tours for credulous tourists. A treasure hunt was an essential part of the experience.

Rat thought this was very funny and so did all the other animals when the word was spread around. They had never cared much about the mythical treasure anyway, and it was just as well that the digging stopped before the whole neighborhood was undermined with holes and tunnels.

Nobody bothered to tell Toad, who continued digging for treasure in his basement for another week.

Chapter four: Toad Sets the World on Fire

The new world that the animals were living in seemed somehow quite different, while being in every way the same. The Wall could have changed everything, but nobody could be sure whether it had really changed anything, or whether it was a good thing or a bad thing. Badger worried that it was turning them too much in upon themselves. The Wide World had been an ever-present annoyance, and sometimes a threat. Now there was never any need to hide. But new ideas and challenges had come from the Wide World, like Badger's books and the railway. Nothing new came in anymore. The antics of the human inhabitants out there had allowed all the animals, including the birds and even some of the insects, to feel comfortably superior to these oversized, clumsy creatures. Now, apart from Toad, there was little to laugh at except the pranks of the baby bunnies.

They had a small world all their own, but what should they do with it? There was the ever-present danger of taking themselves seriously. There were whispers about being the "chosen animals." Badger and Pegasus the barge horse were unusually well-read creatures. And they had both noticed some disturbing tendencies. Badger had received an uninvited visit from a character calling himself the "Head Squirrel," asking for his support in a dispute between squirrel families in an old oak tree. Badger was outraged.

"What do you mean Head Squirrel?" he demanded. "We don't have head squirrels or head anybody here. Anyway, there are thousands of trees, and all the squirrels agreed these real estate problems together before."

The squirrel started explaining that he represented a tree zoning committee, which caused Badger to send him away at once. A committee was the first step on the road to perdition, in his opinion, and Pegasus agreed.

"These committees are springing up everywhere," he said, "The rats have half a dozen of them. And I've noticed something else. Since Toad had that embarrassing fiasco with the Destroyer he has been dressing and acting differently. He talks about his "dignity," whatever that means. Ms Tiggywinkle said he has started ordering staff about in Toad Hall instead of ignoring them, and they don't like it."

Badger started observing Toad more closely. Most animals did not wear clothes at all, and Toad had never been a showy dresser. Now he seemed to have found a hoard of old-fashioned gentlemen's clothes somewhere in the recesses of Toad Hall and paraded himself in a smart tweed suit with a silk cravat, shiny brown boots, a walking cane, and a bowler hat. The result was more ridiculous than impressive, and the little bunnies laughed. But Toad ignored them, holding his nose in the air.

Badger was too polite to comment on this, but he didn't like Toad's new attitude. There was something condescending about it, and this came to a head one day when Toad told Badger to announce a meeting for all the animals in Toad Hall the next Saturday.

"I'm not in charge of your self-promotion, or anything else" snapped Badger. "Ask them yourself." Toad puffed up with indignation, popping several buttons off his stylish waistcoat, and walked out. The Dirty Rat tribe were soon posting notices about this meeting all over the Wild Wood. It was advertised as A New and Better World for All Animals, and created a great deal of excited anticipation in, on, and under the trees.

Pegasus didn't like the sound of it. "Political meetings were a human thing," he mused. "They were a way of confusing people and getting them to follow some leader for some reason they didn't understand. They have no place here among us animals. We never had a leader, and we don't need one now."

Pegasus and Badger made sure to go to the meeting, along with Mole and Water Rat. The big reception room at Toad Hall was packed, and a banners were hung across the ceiling with slogans like "Follow the Great Toad to Freedom," "The Great Toad is Always Right," "All animals are equal but Toad is more equal than others," and a much more propaganda of the same kind.

"I don't like this at all," said Pegasus, I've heard something similar before, when I was listening to all those books in my stable. It was about a farmyard where the pigs threw out the humans and governed the other animals. In the end the pigs turned into people. Do you remember that pig who tried to cheat Toad with fake railway shares? He looked almost human."

The Oracat agreed. "This doesn't end well, in fact or fiction," he said, and returned to his tuna bowl.

"It has to end right here," said Badger grimly. But it didn't end yet. Toad was up on the podium launching into what threatened to be a long speech scattered with phrases like "Only the Great Toad can fix your problems," "What you need in this day and age is a mighty leader like Toad."

The audience was not paying much attention to Toad's rhetoric. He had made the mistake of setting up the refreshment tables at the far end of the hall, so that his entire audience was busy eating with their backs to him and paid very little attention to the speech.

As Toad came to his peroration, with another glowing description of the ideal world to come under the benevolent dictatorship of Toad, they turned back to face him, hoping that more food would be set out when he had finished.

"We will parade around the boundaries of our land to show that it belongs to us, or rather to me," Toad shouted above the sound of munching jaws. "I will lead in my Toadmobile. It will be a spontaneous demonstration of support, so everyone must follow me."

Toad had prepared for this in great detail. He had no fuel for the wrecked and abandoned cars behind Toad Hall, and Pegasus had refused to pull a cart for this embarassing event. So Toad had decided to make a majestic progress around his realm in a steam car, which would be much more dignified than hopping. The ingenious Dirty Rats had been working on this car for weeks. They had used the shell of a long, black limousine that had belonged to Toad's distinguished father, and it stood outside Toad Hall now, puffing smoke and steam and looking rather impressive with Toad's (imaginary) coat of arms painted on both sides.

The animals lined up in a disorderly heap behind the Toadmobile, not at all sure why they were doing this but hoping for more food at the end of it. The procession moved off very slowly at first, partly because the Dirty Rats who were feeding the boiler in the back seat were unhappy about this demeaning work and the miserable pay they were getting from

Toad. But Toad called for more steam, and slowly the speed increased. "This will give those lazy animals a bit of exercise," he thought to himself. "Discipline is what they need." And the Toadmobile moved faster.

Toad never looked back because he thought it would be undignified. A leader must be confident that his followers are following. If he had looked back he would have seen that the accelerating Toadmobile was leaving a trail of smoke and sparks. Most of his followers were coughing, and some had been stung or almost set on fire by the sparks. Small blazes had been ignited in the grass and the hedgerows, and some of the more responsible animals were trying to put them out. Very soon the triumphal procession had disintegrated, with many of the participants quietly sneaking off to Bistro Mole.

Toad rushed on his way, oblivious to the chaos behind him. The rats tending the boiler were singed themselves and quickly abandoned ship. The steam pressure rose, and the Toadmobile moved faster. Toad felt the old mania rising in him and leaned forward over the wheel, forgetting that he was supposed to be leading a dignified procession. Eventually it penetrated his crazed mind that something was wrong. He felt heat on the back of his neck and noticed that his expensive tweed suit was beginning to smoulder. Looking round at last he saw that the whole Toadmobile was ablaze. With a shriek of terror, he leapt from the vehicle and plunged into the ornamental lake, watched ironically by most of the inhabitants of the Wild Wood.

The Toadmobile continued blindly on its way, burning furiously, until it crashed with a fiery explosion into the main entrance of Toad Hall.

Chapter five: Making Willows History

The legend of the Great Toad - which never was much of a legend except to himself - was shattered once and for all. Toad Hall was a smoking ruin, despite the brave efforts of all the animals (except Toad) to save it, and all of Toad's human clothes, furniture, and paraphernalia were gone.

Bruised, singed, and humiliated, Toad went to live in the old castle with Slimena, Ms Tiiggywinkle, the

Hoglets, and the Beavers. It was a strange ménage, but not an unhappy one. Toad, once he had recovered from his burns, seemed like a more reasonable animal. Slimena was almost relieved. She had had enough of aristocratic pretensions of her father, Lord Slimy Toad, and the manic enthusiasms of Toad himself. She rather liked him in his new, subdued state. He no longer dreamed (much) of becoming a great leader, or a racing car driver, or even a rich casino operator. It seemed almost possible (though unlikely) that Toad was growing up.

The charred remains of one of Toad's campaign banners was displayed in Bistro Mole. The end had been burned off, and the surviving part read simply: "All animals are equal." The Old Goat reinforced the message by frequently retelling the story of a fine big mountain goat with splendid horns who wanted to be a king. He lived high in the mountains of France and imagined that he was monarch of all he surveyed, which was a great deal. It was only when he came down from the mountain to impress his subjects with his great size and his splendid horns that he discovered that he was only a goat. This story was told with many sly glances at Toad, who pretended not to hear it.

Now that the animals had no fear of human interference they could live more in the open and behave like themselves, instead of creatures from a nature guidebook. It gave them a great sense of freedom. Mole's Bistro expanded for outdoor dining into what he called Terrasse Mole, and it was always busy in summer. Water rat sculled his little boat up and down the river all day long, always stopping at the old castle for lunch and sometimes climbing up the Oracat's mountain to deliver some cans of tuna and hear what, if anything, Hamish had to say. The ingenious cat had been unusually quiet since The Wall had appeared and seemed to be waiting for something.

The Wall continued to be a subject of fascination and speculation, although now it was accepted as part of their world. But it was an unlovely thing, and the sensitive Water Rat devised a plan to beautify it with a curtain of green shrubs and trees all the way round.

With the help of a team of squirrels he was collecting saplings and cuttings for this big gardening project, which he stored up close to his home and called his "Hedge Fund." Planting was to begin in the autumn.

The Wall never changed, but sometimes it moved back a few inches at night when nobody was looking. These few inches usually revealed nothing but grass, but occasionally there was something else. They found a simple wooden flute, which nobody knew how to play until Slimena showed an unexpected talent for it, enchanting the birds with her ethereal amphibian melodies. There was a colored globe, equally mysterious until Badger deduced that it was a kind of circular map, although a map of what he could not guess. And there was a big, fat book called "A Complete History of the Human Race." It was almost as if these odd things had been placed deliberately alongside the retreating Wall, so that the animals could discover them.

The book looked promising and might answer many questions. The human race was a mystery to most of them. The Old Goat had told many tales of their shocking history, but these were all from a goat's point of view and perhaps a little fanciful. Edward the bear and Henrietta the golden hamster had lived with a family in the Wide World, but their stories of suburban family life were, by contrast, phenomenally dull. Only Pegasus the ex-barge horse had a plain down-to-earth view, and his opinion of the human race was gloomy to say the least, mostly restricted to his life on the towpath and in his stable and soured still further by his radical political opinions.

So, the history book seemed like a treasure for those animals who were curious to know what had gone on outside The Wall in past times. But it was a very long book, full of difficult words that daunted even the Badger. The Old Goat offered to eat it and give them a digest. But he was dissuaded on the grounds that it would certainly give him terrible indigestion. In the end they formed a reading circle and struggled through it, page by page and chapter by chapter, with Emilia Ermine and/or Sally Stoat taking notes.

Less than halfway through Badger threw up his paws while they were still in the middle of the fourteenth century and declared that, instead of depressing themselves with this catalog of horrors, they should be recording and celebrating their own much happier history here in the Wild Wood and on the Riverbank. Nobody argued with this, and the book was put away in Badger's library, which itself had become a kind of museum of the past as there were no longer any new acquisitions from things discarded along the Riverbank.

Badger found the idea of a museum of the past rather appealing, but his own small shelf of literature scarcely added up to anything like a full history. He was dozing one warm afternoon in the Terrace mole, in the chair that had been designated as his special chair and listening to the old goat telling yet another of his stories. When he had first arrived on the Riverbank everyone assumed that the goat's store of tales was unlimited but now they realized that it was not and most of the stories had been heard twenty times over and were beginning to get a bit too familiar, especially the one he was telling now about a goat in the long ago past who had conquered huge parts of Asia, and was known as Alexander the Goat. Animals, like people, enjoy familiar tales, but there are limits. Audience discipline was breaking down, and he was subjected to interruptions especially from the smaller rabbits who cried out things like "You left out the bit about Alexander burning the suet pudding" or "It wasn't like that last time you told it."

This was all very well, badger thought, but it was all about things that had happened long ago and far away, and mostly to goats. So many things had happened here in the Wildwood and along the riverbank in his lifetime that it seemed to pity not to be telling their own stories, and surely that could be managed. There never was such a crowd of loquacious animals, and they certainly had enough stories between them to keep the whole community entertained almost indefinitely.

Everyone loved this idea and could hardly wait to begin. There were practical questions about who would go first, how long they would be allowed to speak, and so on. In a way it was a theatrical enterprise and involved all the problems of ego and staging that any good theatrical event involves. But after a great deal of discussion, it was unanimously agreed that the storytelling would take place on Fridays, one week at Bistro Mole and the next at the Old Castle. The first speaker would be none other than Toad, Badger having declined the honor.

Toad of course was delighted with this mark of recognition. Even in his new relatively humble state he had a high opinion of his own talents and what he saw as his own distinguished history. But the stories he had to tell were so numerous and so long that he was asked to restrict himself to one story per Friday, and on the first Friday he chose to speak not of his pampered early days as a tadpole in a jar at Toad Hall but of his first great adventure that began with a gypsy caravan and ended in jail.

This was a huge success especially the part where Toad was locked up in prison, and the part where he was flung into the river by a washerwoman, and the part where he had to escape in disguise on a train. It was better than any tale they had ever heard, and there was no question that they would want to hear more about the exciting life of their local celebrity. Toad was puffed up with pride as he had been so often in the old days.

In due course the eager audience would hear tales of Toad's second, third, fourth and fifth dangerous escapades, culminating in the fiery crash that had destroyed Toad Hall. He told the stories himself, with many interjections by Slimena who corrected him for lies or exaggeration every few sentences, and sometimes every few words. He told them with an odd mixture of pride and embarrassment, seeing himself perhaps for the first time as others saw him. But before claiming his next moment on the stage he had to wait patiently to hear the stories of all the others.

The water rat was shy at first and unwilling to step forward and tell his story or indeed any one of his many stories. But his beloved River was always in his mind, and he overcame his shyness when it occurred to him that he could tell a sailor's story in verse like one of the epics of olden times. Which he did, to great applause.

It is an ancient Water Rat,
And he stoppeth one of three.
'By thy long grey tail and glittering eye,
Now wherefore stopp'st thou me?

Rat continued in dozens of almost correct stanzas to recount his wild voyage, driven by the wind into the open ocean and stranded (as he thought) on a desert island, insulted by ironical crabs, and rescued at last by Pegasus and the other heroes, and ending on a resounding note:

He went like one that hath been stunned,
And is of sense forlorn:
A sadder and a wiser Rat,
He rose the morrow morn.

This was an especially memorable story because of the verse, and the bunnies immediately began to memorize it, but rarely got beyond the first two lines.

Mole came next and was even more shy about standing up before the assembled company and telling his story. But, in the end, he was persuaded by Emelia Ermine to recount the extraordinary tale of the ghost that had haunted at Toad Hall, and his own brave part in capturing the ghost who turned out to be none other than Emelia herself, the enterprising newspaper reporter moonlighting as a biographer for the eternally self-promoting Toad.

The Oracat was also reticent, claiming that professional ethics prevented him from talking about the lives of his credulous customers. But he set aside his tuna sandwich long enough to regale the crowd with a famous piece of cat history which, like all history, had happened long ago and far away. He claimed to be the latest in a long line of prophetic felines going all the way back to ancient Greece where people traveled to an ancient sacred place in Greece to learn about their futures. The Delphic Oracat was famous all over the world, and, like the modern Oracat himself, was never wrong if you interpreted her prophecies the right way.

Pegasus was a modest horse with far too little to say for himself, but he was persuaded to recount the story of the famous trip to the seaside when he pulled a cart filled with just about all the inhabitants of the Wildwood and the riverbank down to the seashore where they enjoyed an astonishing spectacle of the human animals conducting their so-called holidays on the edge of the water. All the animals who had been on the trip which meant all of them joined in with their own personal reminiscences of that splendid day, and with urgent requests that the adventure should be repeated.

Ms Tiggywinkle, who was also distinguished for her modesty, contented herself with some vivid reminiscences based on her life in the ancient Crusader castle and her friendship with Dennis the Dragon whose memories went even further back. They heard tales of chivalry and derring-do, and tales of romance about knights who rode away to the Crusades for years at a time and then came back to meet their beloved in the castle tower, and then as soon as possible rode away again. "It's all repetition," she said, twinkling merrily at her audience, "Don't let any creature tell you otherwise."

Otter & Portly had one heroic story to tell the day of the great storm when they and they alone were able to carry across the turbulent river a heavy piece of rope which became the basis for a crude ferry and which allowed all the animals to be carried across safely to toad Hall on that terrible nights.

Badger maintained a decent reticence about his own quiet life, although he was persuaded to recall the brave attack on the stoats and weasels who had occupied Toad Hall, in which Badger was the leader. But, apart from that, he contented himself with some useful facts about the history and symbolism of badgers (they symbolized strength and courage) and the ancient British family he came from. In olden times the badger had been called Brock, a respected name. But nobody knew much about the private lives of badgers, and Professor Badger Emeritus of the Wild Wood was happy to leave it that way.

When the turn of the Dormouse came - towards the end of the list because he had joined the community so late - he emerged from his teapot and told a long and improbable story about a tea party he had been to long time ago with some very strange characters at which, according to his own account, he had told a lot of very brilliant and funny stories. However, the Dormouse fell asleep before the end of his tale, so they never heard any of his brilliant and funny stories.

And so it went on week after week with more stories and more repetitions earning more applause until the history of the Wildwood and the riverbank had become something real and important to all its inhabitants. It was a history of their own, not always strictly accurate (because no history ever is), but always entertaining and fun (as real history rarely is). Nobody was left out. The birds sang their stories and the ducks quacked theirs, although the mute swans said nothing. Even the busy beavers found time to offer a hasty talk on carpentry and water conservation. The Willows History was the completest thing, and yet never complete because they added to it every year.

Badger was justifiably proud of this community history in stories. It was, he thought, his *chef d'oevre* (another expression he had picked up from his random reading). It deserved to be immortalized in print, because Badger had always respected and collected printed things, and Emelia Ermine and Sally Stoat were of course writing it down as fast as they could, so nothing would be lost. It was a great achievement. Badger felt he could die happy, although he decided to put this off for a long, long time.

Chapter six - A Musical Interlude

As summer turned into autumn the Water Rat was busy with his new project to circle the community with a beautiful hedge along the inside of The Wall. He alternated small saplings with flowering plants, and bushes, aiming for an effect that would be both artistic and practical. After some thought he left a small opening in the hedge not far from the Hidden Cottage so that those who wanted to come in or go out would not have to fight their way through the foliage. In later years this hedge grew to an impressive height and thickness and became famous in that part of the world. The land enclosed by it would be seen as a special, almost magical place, although nobody outside knew exactly why.

The Hidden Cottage was also a scene of great activity. It was a rambling, ramshackle building with many rooms that seem to multiply the more they were explored. The remaining laboratory rats had decided to take an accurate measurement of the place, and they could be seen scurrying round and round and up and down the cottage, inside and outside, with slide rules, tape measures, and even a theodolite. After holding a scientific seminar on the subject, they announced that the cottage contained an infinite number of rooms. They had arrived at this number by multiplying the number of rooms they had found and measured by the number of rooms they couldn't find but thought must be there somewhere. The other animals, after scratching their heads and doing the arithmetic, agreed that this must be correct.

This exploration produced many surprises, including some inhabitants that nobody had previously known about – some shrews, bats, and a possum who must have escaped from a zoo somewhere - who were welcomed into the community with varying degrees of enthusiasm. But the most exciting discovery was a vast room absolutely packed from floor to ceiling with junk. It was impossible even to get inside, and the beavers had to be called in to gnaw a passage through the heaps. The Beavers were delighted to get their teeth into this treasure house of old furniture made from high quality polished wood. They planned to use it for building superior and more shiny beaver dams.

Many ordinary domestic objects were uncovered during this clearing out of the junk room – including utensils that proved useful to Mole in his kitchen. Some supposedly decorative objects emerged, which were universally rejected as ugly, and an old bicycle which nobody could understand. More interesting was a box with a conical brass horn mounted on top and a handle on the side. It was as much a mystery as the bicycle and, when it had been dusted off and brought out into the daylight, everyone was invited to have a guess about its purpose. Edward the Bear and Henrietta the Hamster had no problem giving it a name. "It's a phonograph," they exclaimed with delight, and everyone was impressed but not much enlightened.

Henrietta explained that the phonograph was for making music, but it was incomplete. In the depths of the junk room she unearthed a dusty heap of objects that needed several animals to get it back outside where it could be cleaned and inspected. It proved to be a pile of thin circular black discs, all with a hole in the middle and a mysterious label. This was a welcome find for Henrietta and Edward who, in their earlier domestic lives, had had been familiar with entertainment devices of this sort. They set to work to get the phonograph going.

The result astonished everybody. They were accustomed to the songs of birds, and the wind in the trees, and even Slimena's strange amphibian performances on the flute. But the Wild Wood had never resounded to the sound of the BBC Symphony Orchestra, and the full-throated voice of a dramatic soprano made some of the birds stretch their eyes.

It wasn't long before Mole added musical evenings to the evening Bistro program. The animals had no idea what they were hearing, but applauded everything equally, from symphonies to jazz. It provided an extra touch of gaiety to what was already a happy scene.

As the year headed towards its close everyone was conscious of the approaching Winter Solstice, not because they had calendars but from untold generations of experience. They knew in their bones that this was an important turning point, which they interpreted to mean that it was time for a party, The old goat confirmed that this was the case all over the world. Everybody on earth down the centuries had found reasons to celebrate at this darkening time of year, and their celebrations, like their reasons, were strange and various.

It was inevitable that the strange and various population of the Wild Wood and the Riverbank would decide to have several parties, just to be sure that they had done the thing right. There was a party in the shade of the trees, a party up in the trees for the birds and squirrels, and a party under the roots of the trees for the burrowing animals. Several parties spread out along the riverbank like a horizontal picnic, and Otter and Little Portly organized a festival in the river itself for the waterfowl and the swimming fraternity. There were parties in the Hidden Cottage and in the Old Castle. There was art and poetry, games and storytelling, the new music, and even a bit of awkward four-legged dancing. It was the most thorough celebration that anyone could remember, and they were exhilarated and exhausted at the end of it.

Through all this joyful activity, as the evenings drew in, Badger had the feeling that they were being watched – not in a sinister way but he had the strangest conviction that they were being judged. But he couldn't tell how or by whom. Pegasus agreed, and the Oracat had an even more dramatic view. "We are being studied by something huge and powerful bigger than all of us," he said, "A great power that has made all these changes and perhaps will make more. We will have to face this mighty being soon."

Having delivered his dire prophecy, which was at least half true, he opened another can of tuna.

Chapter seven: The Mice Rearrange Everything

As the Oracat had more or less predicted, the Mighty and Powerful Being arrived in the Wild Wood a few days later. But she was not noticed at first because she was dozing under one of the outdoor tables on Terrasse Mole.

When she felt thoroughly rested, she gathered all the messenger mice together under the table and gave them instructions. They were told to rouse up every living creature in the community and tell them to gather in front of the Hidden Cottage at noon, to hear a vitally important message. Although some were indignant at being woken up, they had never heard a vitally important message before, or even an unimportant one, so everyone was there on time, full of curiosity.

They couldn't see anything remarkable at first until the messenger mice pointed up and there, on top of a chair balanced on top of one of Mole's dining tables, was a white mouse. She was a pretty thing, very sleek although slightly plump, with pink eyes and a pink nose and pink ears. a pink tail, and pink paws. She waved one of these paws for silence and got it eventually.

"Greetings creatures of the Wild Wood and Riverbank," she began, and although her voice was very small she could be heard perfectly by everyone in the big crowd. "I bring you an important message from the Mistresses of the Universe. I am their spokesmouse. My name is Ethel. Listen very carefully, I shall squeak this only once."

"Don't you mean Masters of the Universe?" cried an irrepressible young bunny.

"Of course not. Don't you know anything?" snapped the Spokesmouse, annoyed at being interrupted before she had even started. "The universe is unimaginably vast, with millions of galaxies and billons of planets like this, and trillions of creatures just like you." She caught a glimpse of Toad and Slimena in the crowd and shuddered slightly. "All these worlds must be watched over and adjusted occasionally. It's a monumental task. The record-keeping mice can scarcely keep up. They tend to go on vacation and not come back."

"So, why are lady white mice the mistresses of the universe?" asked Badger politely, who really wanted to know.

"Nobody else would take the job," replied Ethel, snappishly. "And the boy white mice were too lazy, forever playing silly mouse games and arguing about who won. Now, can we get on?"

"You see, every world is an experiment, and part of this experiment that you call the Wide World went wrong. We didn't keep a close enough eye on the evolution of some monkey-like creatures, and a few million years slipped by before we noticed that they had turned into monsters. They learned to stand up and use their hands, and the first thing they did was to make weapons and fight, and they never stopped. They grew clever and proud, as well as aggressive, and were just on the verge of creating weapons that would destroy everything, animals included. This seemed to be what they wanted, as insane as it sounds. Well we're not having it. No experiment is perfect. We decided to terminate that sector of the testing ground, which was almost all of it except for this little place here and a spot in the Himalayas, and start again without the monkey creatures."

The senior lab rat was delighted that he had guessed the secret of the universe. His colleagues cheered him and dubbed him "Ratstein" forever afterwards. The rabbits set up a chant of "Four legs good two legs bad."

"So," the spokesmouse continued doggedly, ignoring this disturbance, "You may have noticed that we have been doing a bit of housekeeping around here. We got rid of the Wide World and temporarily replaced it with...."

"Anti-matter," cried the lab rats, now very pleased with themselves.

"No, anti-matter is hard to find and expensive. We replaced it with nothing. Nothing is cheap and plentiful. A group of American rats found an enormous amount of nothing in a place called Washington, so we just brought it here and spread it around, and before long everything was nothing."

The spokesmouse Ethel was not accustomed to animals who were curious and articulate. Usually they just squeaked or grunted, which was fine with her. But now there were questions from all sides.

Q. "What happened to the people in the Wide World? Were they upset?"

A. "They noticed nothing, because nothing happened, that's the whole point. Now we will create something new and less dangerous, and you will find yourselves living in a much better neighborhood. That's about it. Simple enough. A whole new world, all yours."

Q. What happened to all the animals?

A. They have been put into comfortable storage, and will be back as good as new – although a few of them had to be sent to MHQ for re-education. We are not naïve, after managing an unruly universe for millions of years. Some creatures had bad habits. Now they will all be vegetarians.

Q. How did you do that?

A. It was hard to retrain some of the carnivores, to be honest. There was some risk of being eaten ourselves. So instead of changing them we changed their food. The animals that were prey now taste like cabbage or broccoli, and so they are safe from carnivores. If you see a tiger eating salad, for example, it's because it tastes like his favorite meat dish. It was tricky, but our nutrition specialists managed it

Q. Will all these new animals be like us?

A. Well, no, there will be some animals you have never met, like aardvarks and zebras, but they will be far away getting on with their own lives.

Q. Will there be rabbits?

A. Of course, lots of rabbits. The universe is overrun with rabbits. There may soon be nothing but rabbits. (This produced a cheer from the rabbits.)

Q. Will there be toads?

A. Yes, I'm afraid so, but without humans to imitate toads will be somewhat more sensible, although still just as ugly.

Q. How long have White Mice been doing this?

A. We took it over millions of years ago from cats, who were always asleep on the job. I must admit that our early efforts at world-building were rather cheesy, but everything's under control now.

Q. How has the truth about the power of White Mice been hidden?

A. The secret had almost slipped out once or twice but nobody wanted to believe it. We put out a lot of disinformation about gods and saints and things which the monkey creatures turned into religions. We disguised ourselves as pets and Lab mice, in order to make observations. It's only lady White Mice, you understand (holding up a pink paw for emphasis) – regular mice are just mice, and boy mice of any color are useless.

Q. Why are you doing this now?

A. The monkey creatures had almost put our evolution plan into reverse. They were heading back towards barbarism, and working on weapons that would soon have taken them all the way. This was the last chance before they destroyed everything from pole to pole. (Water Rat wondered briefly about the location of these poles, but didn't want to miss any of this).

Q. What will the new Wide World be like?

A. Exactly like this, but better.

Q. What should we do in this new world?

A. Just do what you've always done – eating and sleeping and having fun. Nobody knows what animals *should* be doing, or why we exist at all. That information is above my pay grade, but I suspect that the answer is that nobody has the slightest idea, and it's best not to ask.

Q. Why was Wild Wood saved?

A. You fellows have done pretty well. You are happy, creative, kind to one another, sometimes silly but mostly sensible (again a sharp look at Toad), and you try not to do any harm. You have no leaders, princes, priests, presidents, aristocrats, or chief executives, and you never start a war. That's about as good as it gets in this or any other world.

There was a pause, in which the animals looked at one another with quiet satisfaction.

"No more questions? Good," she said with relief. "This adjustment will take a while, but there's no rush. I suggest you all have a nice long nap and see what you find when you wake up. It may be confusing at first, but I hope you like it." And the white mouse vanished in a puff of pink smoke, leaving a stunned silence that went on and on until Mole banged the gong for lunch.

The snow began soon afterwards, soft and steady and apparently endless. All the animals settled down to sleep, even those who never hibernated like the horse and the goat, and they all soon vanished under the deep white blanket. A great deal of time passed in complete silence. Then, one day without a date, the snow began to melt, and life stirred in the Wild Wood again.

The White Wall had vanished, along with the snow. The sun rose on a broad green vista of meadows and great forests, that certainly had not been there before. No buildings, roads or railways disfigured the landscape, and the sky was as clear as glass. Millions of animals woke up not knowing that this was their first day of their first spring. They took it all for granted, and just got on with their lives in the usual way.

In the Wild Wood and along the Riverbank the animals stirred, and blinked, and thought about their extraordinary dream. Hibernation often brought strange dreams, but this dream about White Mice who were mistresses of the universe was beyond anything they could have imagined. But there's nothing to be done about dreams except to laugh and let them fade away. Everything looked the same, except for the fine flowering hedge that surrounded their whole territory where the Wall had been, and that was certainly an improvement. It was the beginning of a new year, and there were things to be done.

Chapter eight: The First Spring

The Mole had been working very hard all morning spring cleaning his little home, first with brooms, then with dusters, then on ladders and steps and chairs, with a brush and a pale of whitewash, until he had dust in his throat and eyes, and splashes of whitewash all over his black fur, and an aching back and weary arms. Spring was moving in the air above and in the earth below and all around him, penetrating even his dark and lonely little house with its spirit of divine discontent and longing. It was small wonder then that he suddenly flung down his brush on the floor and said, "blow" and also "hang spring cleaning" and bolted out of the house without even waiting to put on his coat. Something up above was calling him imperiously, and he made for the steep little tunnel which answered in his case to the graveled carriage driver owned by animals whose residences are nearer to the sun and air. So he scraped and scratched and scrabbled and Scrooged, and then he Scrooged again, and scrabbled and scratched and scraped working busily with his little paws and murmuring to himself "up we go, up we go" until at last "pop" his snout came out into the moonlight into the sunlight and he found himself rolling in the warm grass of a great Meadow.

This is fine, he said to himself, this is better than whitewashing. The sunlight struck hard on his fur, soft breezes caressed his heated brow and after the seclusion of the burrow he had lived in so long the call of happy birds fell on his dull ear almost like a shout. Jumping off all his four legs at once with the joy of living and the delight of spring without its cleaning, he pursued his way across the meadow until he reached the hedge on the farther side.

It all seemed too good to be true, as he rambled busily along the hedgerows, across the copses, finding everywhere birds building, flowers budding, leaves thrusting, everything happy and progressive and occupied. He thought his happiness was complete when, as he meandered aimlessly along, suddenly he stood by the edge of a full fed River.

This was a delightful surprise, and yet somehow it was the most familiar and friendly place in the world. He had been here before. Across the water there was a hole in the riverbank where he could see a pair of bright eyes looking at him. A small face gradually grew up around the eyes, like a frame around a picture. A little brown face with whiskers. A grave round face, with the same twinkle in the eye that had first attracted his notice. Small ears and thick silky fur. It was the Water Rat.

"Ratty" cried Mole in delight. "There you are. I seem to have been asleep for so long that I had almost forgotten. But how could I?"

"Moley" cried the Rat, equally delighted. "I was beginning to think that I was the only creature awake in the world. But look, here are some ducks too," as a family paddled by, the ducklings in a neat line. "How splendid it is to see you. Do you know what happened? Did you have a strange dream about White Mice? Have you seen Badger and the others?"

The flurry of questions and answers was too much to continue across the breadth of the river, so the Water Rat launched his little boat, sculled over to Mole's side, and soon they were heading down stream together as they had so often in another time, asking each other "Do you remember?" "Do you remember?" at every new sight along the Riverbank. The ruins of Toad Hall and the tower of the old castle brought floods of memories.

The mysterious white Wall had entirely disappeared, and the Water Rat's newly planted hedge was now so dense and tall, with well-grown trees at intervals, that they could scarcely see the landscape beyond. How could it have grown so big in a single winter? They wondered but found no answers. "Everything seems a little odd," said Mole thoughtfully, "But so far there's nothing bad. I ought to be in my Bistro if it's still there. Let's go to the Hidden Cottage and see who else is awake."

They tied up the boat and, with some trepidation, not knowing what they would find, headed into the Wild Wood towards the Cottage. They found that everybody was wide awake and waiting impatiently for their breakfasts after a long hibernation.

"You know Moley," said Rat, laughing, "You have upset the balance of nature here. Animals used to get their own food, not line up at a buffet."

"Phooey," said Mole, who was much too busy greeting and serving his customers to discuss such abstract things. "Nature *is* a buffet, I have just organized it more conveniently."

A cheer went up from the crowded tables as Badger appeared, still blinking sleepily, and took his usual place. By the time breakfast was over and the animals were beginning to think about lunch, everything seemed almost normal. Badger was quietly pleased with his reception, but obscurely felt that something should be said or done to mark this very unusual day. But what?

After the meal the more thoughtful animals gathered around Badger. Pegasus and the Old Goat were there. Ms Tiggywinkle soon appeared and reported that all was well at the castle. The Hoglets were flourishing and the Beavers were at work on a superior dam made out of Victorian furniture. The Oracat slipped into the cottage at the last minute, trying not to be noticed. All eyes inevitably turned in his direction and could hardly fail to see that he was followed by a charming kitten, black with a white bib and a white tip to her tail, who nobody had ever seen before. The Oracat blushed, insofar as an orange cat can blush.

"I don't know where she came from," he said hastily. "She was just there when I woke up." The Orakitten sat down and began to wash her paws. After a blank moment in which curiosity struggled with good manners, the animals went back to their meeting.

Toad did not join this gathering. He was sitting in the tower of the old castle, which was now his home, gazing wistfully out at the broad new landscape, wondering if his magnificent Destroyer vehicle was out there somewhere. It had vanished through the Wall at full speed, and it couldn't keep running forever, but there was no sign of it. Toad sighed.

Slimena, who was already tired of Toad's nostalgia for the old world, was down by the river fishing without a hook. This was not a very satisfying occupation but Slimena, being an amphibian, regarded fish as distant relatives, and certainly not as potential dinner. So she indulged in this fishless fishing out of sheer borebom. When her boredom reached an intolerable pitch, she abandoned her pole and net and hopped over to the Hidden Cottage, where the others were having their conference. They had all slept for a long, long time, they had all had strange dreams about White Mice, and they were all rather confused.

"First of all," Badger began, with his usual sturdy common sense, "We know who we are. We have our stories, and everybody remembers them. We have the Wild Wood and the Riverbank, and our history, so nothing important has been lost. But the Wide World seems to have changed completely, as far as we can see through the hedge, and the question is: what happened, and what should we do about it?"

Two schools of opinion quickly emerged. One (the majority) said that they should do nothing, go nowhere, and carry on as if nothing had happened because, according to the White Spokesmouse Ethel, nothing *had* happened to the Wide World. The others, refusing to accept this metaphysical spin, argued that it was essential as well as irresistible to find out more about the new World that surrounded them.

Ms Tiggywinkle was firmly of the opinion that they should do nothing. "It's all repetition, just as I told you," She explained with a reassuring smile. "The world is starting again, it happens all the time, and we should just carry on as usual."

"But where are we starting *from,*" cried the anxious Mole. "If we are starting from the beginning of time there will be dinosaurs and things out there beyond the hedge."

"No, no," said Ms Tiggywinkle soothingly. "We must be starting again from exactly where we were. The Hidden Cottage is still here, although now we don't have to hide from human beings we should call it Obvious Cottage, We are all still here so, as Mr. Badger said nothing important has changed.

Just at that moment, the outside world paid a visit in the form not of a dinosaur but of a handsome family of deer who stepped delicately through the hole in the Hedge and stared with their big, gentle eyes at the assembled animals. The buck, with his fine antlers, came first, followed by a beautiful doe and a tiny, speckled fawn. Badger was the first to recover from the general amazement and welcomed the newcomers graciously. They would obviously be a valuable source of information. The deer, who were bewildered by finding themselves in such an unexpected and exotic company, seemed willing to answer any and all questions, but unsure of any precise facts. All animals had been given the gift of language, it seemed, but not necessarily the gift of fluency, or even common sense.

"How are things out to the west?" asked Badger, pointing in the direction the deer had come from. "It's very nice," they said, and went on to confirm that every place they had visited at every point of the compass was "fine" or "very nice." Nobody shot at them, they said, no cars ran them down, and there was more fresh food than they could possibly eat. The fawn made a contribution, speaking more confidently than her parents. "It's so much fun out there" she enthused, "Lots of lovely deer to play with, some almost as pretty as my mother." This earned her a warm smile from mother, an irritable shake of the antlers from father, and a glare from Slimena who said: "So it's a beauty contest out there, is it.?"

Mole asked them about some old rumors that Wide World people had cultivated what they called "gardens" full of all kinds of succulent treats that deer loved. But they had never heard about any such charitable act. "It sounds very nice," they said, "But we have always found our own food." Their eyes nevertheless drifted towards the remains of the lunch buffet in Bistro Mole.

The debate continued and, as always happens in a genuine democracy, no definite conclusion was reached. But before dinner was served it was clear that a small group of explorers would have to go out into the new Wide World and come back with more useful descriptions than the Deer could offer, and the rest would stay home and enjoy themselves, just as the spokesmouse had recommended.

The adventurous Old Goat volunteered to lead the expedition. "We will never feel safe until we know what is out there," he repeated, and the animals who planned to stay safely at home agreed with relief. Toad was full of enthusiasm for an expedition that might rediscover his lost world of fast cars and policemen, although he had no intention of going himself. But the Old Goat, in spite of his age, was ready for another travel adventure. "I will need some backup," he said, "I never was very young and now I'm not as young as I used to be. A bird would be ideal – birds can see a long way." Right on cue Maggie the Magpie strutted forward. "I have great eyesight," she claimed, "and I'm a good talker if we meet anybody to talk to and, in any case, I'm getting fat here and need the exercise."

Everybody agreed that the William the Goat and the Maggie Magpie would make a perfect exploration team, and they soon set off through the gap in the hedge to the sound of cheering, after which the relieved animals got back to their small domestic tasks and instantly forgot about the mysterious New World that now surrounded them.

But they would never forget that First Spring, at least not until the even more memorable events of the First Summer.

Chapter nine: Headline News

Spring flowered along the Riverbank and, as usual, the animals took full advantage of it. They remembered the parting advice of the spokesmouse to "enjoy yourselves," and never had any piece of advice been so welcome or so easy to follow. Most of them gave little thought to the bold explorers out there in the great unknown, although their particular friends were anxious. After a long period of waiting, the Old Goat and the Magpie returned from their expedition, looking plump and satisfied. The goat reported that the new world was a splendid place with lots of vegetation to eat, but rather dull, and with animals far less articulate and lively than those here in the Wild Wood. He missed the drama and chaos that he had seen in his travels before and that all his tribe had reported from the earliest times. "Nothing disgusting or horrible happens without human beings," he complained, "A goat could get bored out there."

The Magpie had nothing but praise for the new Wide World. Of course, like the Badger, the Magpie tended to see things in black and white. "It's a kind of primitive paradise," she enthused, and it was clear that there was nothing to be afraid of, except perhaps the tedium that is inseparable from any paradise. The baby bunnies started making little forays beyond the hedge, and all came back safely, not that anyone was counting.

The only discontent was in the office of *The Riverbank Record,* now established in one of the numerous spare rooms of the renamed Obvious Cottage, where Sally Stoat and Emilia Ermine, separately and together, lamented the strange turn of events that had deprived them of all their best material.

"I never realized it before," said Emilia, "But our best stories always came either from outside in the Wide World, or from Toad. Now there are no human beings to create problems for us, and Toad has gone strangely quiet. Nobody gets excited by headlines like **Squirrels Find More Acorns** or **Ducks Report Damp Conditions in River.** This could be terrible for our circulation."

Their desire for a larger circulation was not a matter of greed but of pride. *The Riverbank Record* was a labor of love for the two reporters. The paper was distributed free to everyone who wanted it, and often to those who did not. Some animals read it, some had it read to them, some made nests out of it, and some ate it. It was a matter of pride for Sally and Emilia to report the most interesting and dramatic stories of the community for everyone.

Sally Stoat agreed that they were in danger of losing their readership. She could hardly not agree, both of them being one and the same reporter, as well as the editor and proprietor of the paper. "But we can't go out and cover the whole of the New Wide World, just the one of us. We don't even know how big it is, or whether they will be able to read the *Record* out there." (*The Riverbank Record* was published in what they hopefully called UAL or Universal Animal Language, but they didn't know how universal it was).

"I hate to say this," said Sally, but saying it, "But that leaves us with nothing but Toad. If he doesn't do something outrageous soon *The Riverbank Record* will expire from lack of interest."

They thought about what makes a good news story. Crimes, disasters, explosions, fires, accidents, any kind of conflict or disagreement, disappointment, humiliation, or failure. All of these pointed straight to Toad. Having contemplated this list they went to interview him in The Castle where he was now living. They found him still gazing out sadly at what was, for him, a deeply uninspiring landscape – nothing but pure nature as far as the eye could see. He was happy to talk to the binary journalists for a change, now in the process of adopting their summer identity as Sally Stoat. They had been working on and off (mostly off) for a long time on Toad's memoirs. He had never been allowed to see the work in progress but imagined it as something overwhelmingly flattering that would establish forever his reputation as the Great Toad. In fact the pair had been injecting so much fiction, fantasy, and sly humor into the narrative that it was more likely to make him a universal joke. But they were not here to discuss such uncomfortable things.

"Are you quite well, Toad?" asked Sally. to start the conversation. Toad was startled. Nobody ever asked him if he was quite well. He never even asked himself.

"Of course, in the pink," he replied, which was not strictly true because he was, as always, a sickly greenish-brown color.

"Well, you have been so quiet," Sally pursued. "You haven't stolen ay cars, exploded any yachts or burned down any houses for months now."

"I've been busy," said Toad, puffing himself up. They let a silence grow while Toad tried to think of what had kept him busy.

"It's boring," he exploded at last. "Everything is boring. There's nothing to do and nowhere to go and no motor vehicles to get there in."

"Why don't you go looking for the great Destroyer," urged Sally, "Or get the Dirty Rats to put something together from the wrecks behind your old house? A Toad without a motor car is a sad spectacle."

"Oh, it's all very well to talk," moaned Toad. The Dirty Rats are not very cooperative these days – they got singed by my last experiment. And I don't know where we could find any motor fuel. It's a desert out there, and Pegasus refuses to help this time."

"Mr. Toad," said Sally Stoat, aiming for a suitably respectful and flattering tone, "You are the most distinguished personage in our Riverbank community, the star in fact. Your bold exploits, and the repairs and recovery afterwards, have filled the pages of The Riverbank Record, and our readers miss them. Do consider what a story it would be if you bravely went out into the New Wide World all alone in search of your motor car. Perhaps you could drive it back in triumph. Don't let the Old Goat get all the glory."

"But what about the monsters?" muttered Toad.

Rumors like this have a way of being both true and not true at the same time. This one was the fault of the Magpie, who had flown much further and faster than the Old Goat could walk. From her great height he had seen some strange sights, including a group of unusual animals of all shapes and sizes, some very big, none of which had ever been seen in the Wild Wood community. Maggie Magpie had kept quiet about this when the expedition first returned so as not to cause alarm, but not quiet enough. She whispered what he had seen to her friends in the Frequent Flyers Club and urged them to keep it secret. But a Magpie's whisper is too loud for a secret, and the news spread fast, gathering colorful details all the time, until there was a diffuse anxiety about "monsters" in the whole community. This anxiety had reached Toad, and worked on his imaginative, volatile nature.

He sent the reporters away with a promise to think about it, and he thought about it. On the one hand he would love some good publicity in *The Riverbank Record.* On the other he didn't want to wear himself out hopping all over the country only to be eaten by monsters. He thought for a long time, and then hopped over to the burnt-out ruins of Toad Hall. As he had remembered the basement, sturdily built (as he claimed) by his great-great-great grandfather many years ago, was largely intact, although somewhat infested with Dirty Rats and Rabbits. Toad returned to the Castle and put his plan into operation.

A week was spent in secret preparations, and then he sent a messenger mouse to *The Riverbank Record* announcing that he had changed his mind and was ready to depart on his own solitary, heroic expedition into the unknown exterior, as soon as a reporter could be sent to the castle to record the event.

The very next day, surrounded by a hastily-gathered crown of cheering animals, he was on his way, dressed in what he considered to be proper expedition style with a sunhat, a walking staff, large boots and a huge pack of supplies on his back that he called the "ToadBag." He followed the path taken by the vanished Destroyer car, and soon vanished into the woods.

Slimena watched him go with satisfaction, and just a tinge of anxiety. The reporter Sally Stoat watched him go with suspicious eyes. There was something odd about Toad's sudden decision to take this risk and Sally, like the dedicated reporter she was, determined to get the true story.

Toad kept walking until he was well out of sight of the Castle and then collapsed on the grass and took a nap. As dusk fell, he crept back to the ruins of Toad Hall and slithered into the basement where he had arranged a very comfortable little apartment for himself. "Am I not a clever Toad to outwit all these silly animals?" he thought as he fell asleep. "Toad is not stupid enough hop for miles through the wilderness and get himself eaten by monsters. Toad is still the smartest and the greatest!"

Chapter ten: Toad Has Two Secrets

The headline in the next day's *Riverbank Record* was all that Toad could have wished. **HEROIC TOAD PURSUES MYSTERY MONSTERS.** It was a public relations triumph, and many Riverbankers began to think about Toad more charitably. These forgiving souls did not include Hamish the Oracat, who smiled ironically when he read the news report.

Hamish had established his Grotto of Enlightenment on top of the highest hill in the neighborhood. He had sharp eyesight and could watch practically everything that went on along the Riverbank, night or day. He had followed Toad's conspicuous departure from the Castle, his short hike into the woods, and his return and dusk to slither into the basement of the Toad Hall ruins. The Oracat could guess what was coming, but he decided to keep this knowledge to himself for a while.

All was not well with the Oracat. He needed a break from the prophecy business, and he needed a stroke of luck. The transformation of his community into something like a terrestrial paradise had sharply cut down on the number of anxieties and neuroses that provided him with a steady flow of customers. What was worse the newly arrived Orakitten, now named Oracula, had shown unexpected gifts in the prophecy line, so that female animals with a problem tended to come to her for reassurance. The Oracat himself always dismissed female problems unsympathetically as "mimsies" or "megrims" or "vapours." The Orakitten had a more delicate touch. As the clients flowed in her direction, so did the supply of Tuna, which was already running low. It was an uncomfortable situation, but not for her.

The Orakitten sat comfortably with her white tipped paws folded in front of her and her green eyes wide open.

"Why don't we move the consulting room to the Obvious Cottage? She asked, not for the first time. "It would be much more convenient for everybody."

The Oracat had learned to dread questions beginning "Why don't we?" suggesting as they did that this was a joint enterprise. He had always been a solitary cat and had no notion of starting some kind of group practice, and he needed his high perch to keep an eye on things below and maintain his reputation for knowing everything.

"It's not a consulting room, it's a Grotto of Enlightenment," he grumbled. "Consulting is a therapy not a solution, it may not come up with the right answer. A genuine Oracle like me always gives the right answer, if only the client understands it properly. Reaching the Grotto is part of the experience. If you have to climb all the way up here on a freezing wet day you are likely to value the advice you get much more. Consulting room – phooey."

So saying the Oracat went to sleep. The Orakitten also closed her eyes. She could wait for him to change his mind. Cats are good at waiting.

The return of Toad from his imaginary expedition a few days later was predictably farcical. He staggered into the Obvious Cottage at the busiest time, just before lunch, his boots muddy and his clothes tattered. His face might have been smudged with dirt but, given his normal complexion, it was hard to tell.

Toad collapsed on a chair and called for food, which the rabbits willingly brought although this was supposed to be a self-service establishment. Everyone gathered around to hear his story, including the Oracat, who was here for lunch because Mole controlled the tuna supply. The cynical cat could hardly wait to hear what fantasies Toad would have invented about his travels in the New World, and he was not disappointed.

As always, when Toad had an audience, his imagination ran away with him. Based on Maggie Magpie's aerial observations, Toad conjured up a gallery of monsters – huge gray things as big as a house, gigantic cats with stripes, lumbering creatures like tanks with a single horn like a unicorn, and incredibly tall creatures whose necks reached up to the sky. Toad let it be understood that all these monsters and more had tried to eat him, pursued him for miles through field and forest, and only abandoned the chase when the cunning Toad had found refuge in a providential pond.

The young bunnies were immensely excited by this account and showed their unfortunate tendency to Toad worship by a chant of "Hail Toad," which was swiftly suppressed by Badger. "They would start a Toad religion if they could," he muttered to himself. "I'll have to keep an eye on them."

Toad eventually went back to the Castle, where he was coolly greeted by Slimena who had her own doubts about what he had been doing while he was away. In fact Toad had made good use of his time in the basement of Toad Hall. He had made his peace with the Dirty Rats, who had been outraged by his catastrophic handling of the Toad Hybrid, the

Toadmobile and the Destroyer. Some of them still had bald patches where their fur had been singed off. But the Dirty Rats were bored. They were interested only in things mechanical, just as their brothers the Lab Rats in the Obvious Cottage were interested only in things chemical. Toad had a scheme that would engage both groups in a single grand rat project, while confirming Toad's own reputation as a great hero.

Life along the Riverbank settled back into its usual placid routines, defined by dawn and dusk, breakfast, lunch, and dinner. The annual spring festival, which had sprung into existence without anyone planning or organizing it, would have run entirely to schedule if there had been any schedule. As it was the usual happy chaos prevailed. The central event of the festival was a kind of circus, performed in the open space in front of the Obvious Cottage. The literal high point of the circus was an acrobatic act by the squirrels high in the trees called the "The Birdseed Challenge." The birds arranged their feeders (supplied by Bistro Mole) in the most difficult and complicated places, with all kinds of barriers and traps to keep the squirrels away. The squirrels performed astonishing acrobatics to get at the seeds, and usually won. The spectacle attracted large crowds, who usually ended the performance with stiff necks after peering up for so long.

Equally popular was an almost-indescribable show put on by the rabbits called "Bunnynonsense." This involved the performance by all the rabbits (a great number) of a play that nobody could understand because half of it took place underground and all the dialogue was in the incomprehensible language called Bunnyspeak. There was music from the old phonograph, and dancing, and much silliness. Everyone agreed that the show could scarcely be improved.

There were other more serious attractions, including an art exhibit with poems by Water Rat and a cooking demonstration by Mole, who showed an awestruck audience how to make plain, undressed lettuce salad

But the threat of the Monsters was always in the background, and the brave Water Rat, who had not believed Toad's stories at all, decided it was time to find out where and what these monsters were. In the end he didn't have far to go. The monsters came to him.

Chapter 11 – Conversation with a Bear

The water rat was patrolling along his Great Hedge. He had planted the whole thing himself, with the help of a few rabbits and squirrels, and he was sinfully proud of it even though both pride and sin had been abolished. The hedge extended all around the Wildwood and the Riverbank marking the boundary where the mysterious White Wall had once isolated them from the outer World. Now the hedge was tall and rich with plants and bright flowers and substantial trees, and the rat loved to walk all the way round at least once a week, inside and out, to make sure that nothing was damaged or needed his attention.

He had no secateurs, but he did have sharp teeth and trimmed the errant branches as he went along.

He wanted his hedge to look good from both sides. But now, on the outside, he felt slightly exposed and uneasy. How much could he believe of Toad's ridiculous account of Monsters. It sounded like a fantasy, but anything was possible, and out here the rat was vulnerable to any Monsters who might come along. He kept his eyes open as he walked around, noticing that, here and there, somebody else had nibbled at the Hedge with sharp teeth. He suspected the deer who had paid them a visit earlier. In spite of their innocent appearance and polite manners the deer were obviously very interested in food. But the hedge was big enough to spare a few leaves and, in any case, there wasn't much Water Rat could do about it.

Suddenly, he caught his paw on the sharp thorn. It hurt and he uttered an obscure Water Rat malediction as he sat down to suck on it, thinking he was alone But was startled to hear a deep voice behind him ask: "Can I help with that?" He jumped straight into the air turning around at the same time and found himself looking at a large friendly face covered in brown fur. "Sorry if I startled you," said the face, "but I see you have hurt yourself, and I am a Medical Bear."

Rat could see that he was a bear, very similar to their friend Edward, but much larger. Unlike Edward he wore a stethoscope and carried a small black bag marked MB. But he seemed friendly.

"Are you a Monster?" Ask water rat, looking up at the bear and quavering slightly but trying to be brave.

"What an extraordinary idea," said the Bear, somewhat offended. "There are no monsters around here, this is a nice neighborhood."

"But we heard there was a whole herd of strange Monsters over in that direction," said Rat, pointing. And he repeated, in rather less colorful terms, the tale that Toad had told after his return.

The bear laughed in a deeply amused way. "You say a Toad told you this? Toads are the most unreliable creatures in the entire universe. We wouldn't even allow them in our zoo. I see there is some explaining to be done so let's sit down and I will tell you about my friends and you can tell me about yours."

They sat side by side on the grass beside the Hedge, the big bear and the little Water Rat, an amusing sight if anyone had been there to see it. Water Rat, now much reassured, listened attentively to the Bear's narrative.

"In you probably don't know about the zoos," he began, "but they were a kind of prison invented by human beings to keep animals as an entertainment. All the animals that your crazy Toad told you about are from one small zoo. When the Mice cleaned up the human world the zoos everywhere just disappeared, and the animals were liberated. All the farm animals too – cows and sheep and pigs and goats and chickens. We have been trying to settle into a whole new world where nobody is trying to put us in cages, shoot us, or eat us. It takes some getting used to. Many of us in the zoo came originally from barbarous places like Africa or America, but we've all changed now. The mice changed us, cured us of aggression and all kinds of other vices. So you don't need to be afraid of us. Now, let me take a look at that paw of yours. Oh, it's nothing, I'll just bandage it. You don't need insurance," said the Medical Bear reassuringly. "Every treatment is free, whether it works or not," and both of them obligingly laughed at his little joke.

The water rat looked at his neatly bandaged paw and asked "Do you Mons..I mean do you former zoo residents have a leader."

"No, that was one of the first things the Mice cured us of. We are all good friends, and we like to stay together. But nobody is in charge, although some of us are certainly smarter than others," he added, tapping his brown forehead significantly. Now you can tell me about the place you come from, which I presume is on the other side of that beautiful hedge."

Rat scarcely knew where to start. "Well, this is a very quiet and undisturbed part of the country," he explained, "And it has been that way for a long, long time. There's the Wild Wood, and the Riverbank, and they provide everything that anyone could possibly need. So the animals here are a community, perhaps like your zoo friends, even though we are all different (except the rabbits, who are all the same he thought privately,), and we have our habits and rituals through the year. There was a time when human beings disturbed us, but that's over now. Perhaps it is like a zoo without cages, but we all love it here and we are very happy. We have only two rules: one, no violence, and two, respect Mr. Badger. That seems to be enough. Only the animal I mentioned before, Mr. Toad, causes a disturbance sometimes, but we're used to him and he makes us laugh."

The bear was thoughtful. "It sounds like a wonderful place," he mused, gazing through the hedge," and we wouldn't interfere for the world. It is astonishing what you wild animals have accomplished."

Rat was indignant. "What do you mean wild animals?" he asked, sharply. "I am a celebrated poet and painter, my friend Mole is almost a celebrity chef..."

The bear apologized profusely. "Obviously I have got it all wrong," he said. "It must be from spending too much time around humans so we are to some extent humanized." He waved his stethoscope apologetically. "Some of our tigers, for example, are just like domestic pussy cats. You fellows seem to be, how shall I say, more natural, except perhaps for this Toad. We will all have to come to an understanding, and that will be easy now that you and I have met. Goodbye now, take care of that paw." The bear lumbered off.

Water Rat completed the tour of his hedge in a daze and, at the Obvious Cottage, sought out Mole and Badger. They retreated to a quiet corner, where Water Rat showed his bandaged paw and Told his story, with as little exaggeration as possible, to an attentive audience.

"This seems to be very good news," said Badger, judiciously. He had identified and named some of these creatures from a book in his library and learned about their habits, although from a prejudiced human point of view. This knowledge made them less frightening. "It seems that these "monsters" of Toad's are animals just like us, only bigger. If we speak the same language and behave politely to one another, why, we have a whole world to share between us. There shouldn't be any difficulty. The only thing is we can't be very hospitable. The large ones wouldn't fit into the Obvious Cottage, and they would eat up our food supply in no time." This idea alarmed Mole, who looked very thoughtful. Would the Hedge be any defense against hungry monsters? He thought not. It must be friendship or nothing.

At this point there was a distant sound like a small explosion, that shook the cottage, and a few moments later one of the laboratory rats came staggering past with his spectacles awry and smudges of soot on his white coat.

"We must have a word with those Lab Rats, grumbled Mole. They have some messy, smelly, dangerous experiment going on, and it's far too close to my Bistro. They may blow us all up if we don't persuade them to do their testing outside." Everyone agreed and Badger promised to talk severely to the Lab Rats. Then they returned to the main topic.

Pegasus the barge horse had been listening quietly so far, with his head through the window. He knew all about big animals, and had no fear of them.

"It seems to me," he said, "That we should all stay here inside the Hedge, where we are happy and we know everybody, and ask the zoo animals and the farm animals to respect our boundary. We have the Wild Wood, and the River, and the ocean, and the Oracat's mountain. It should be enough for us, if not for Toad. The other animals can visit occasionally if they like but, as Badger says, they are too big to fit into our community. I will act as liaison, an ambassador if you like, because we need to talk to them. But I would like to stay in the Obvious Cottage with the Old Goat. It's become like home to me."

Once again there was enthusiastic agreement. Once more they had reached the perfect solution – which was to do nothing.

So the zoo animals slowly spread throughout the countryside, finding habitats that suited their living habits, and occasionally startling the locals. A ferret, for example, living quietly in the south of England, does not expect to encounter an elephant. But the elephants were always polite, and careful where they put their big feet. The White Mice watched the new world come to life, and were satisfied. But they failed to notice what Toad was up to.

Chapter twelve: The Wandering Weasel

Badger had a surprise visitor, a lady weasel. The great battle of Toad Hall, in which stoats and weasels had been driven out of Toad's home by the furious Badger and his friends, was part of the local folklore. There had been a slight coolness towards stoats and weasels even since, even including the binary Sally Stoat/Emelia Ermine combo who ran, edited, and reported for *The Riverbank Record*. But, as far as Badger was concerned, it was all long forgotten and forgiven, and he welcomed Mrs. Weasel cordially, although with some surprise.

She was nervous. "I wouldn't dream of troubling you Mr. Badger," she began, "But it's my son Wally, he's run away."

"Run away to sea?" asked Badger, thinking that this sounded more like the notion of a young rat than a young weasel.

"No, it's worse, he's run away to be a journalist," cried his unhappy mother. She really was quite pretty in her distress and had even put on a necklace for this visit to the distinguished Mr. Badger. She had thought about a hat but decided it would be too much. Weasels in hats tend to attract adverse comments from other animals.

The story came out in fits and starts and squeaks.

"Wally is a good boy," she said, "He even learned to read from some old newspapers you gave him". She said this with a touch of resentment, but then hurried on. "He became fascinated with those two journalists Sally Stoat and Emelia Ermine, and the reporting they had done on the events in the Wild Wood and along the Riverbank. He said that there was one great story that was not being reported and that was the story of the monsters outside the Hedge, and that he was going to report it himself, and become famous like Sally and Emelia. And off he went early this morning without another word, and I haven't heard from him since."

Badger was worried. In this delicate time the disappearance of any creature was a matter of concern, let alone a youngster like Wally the Weasel. He wasted no time in calling the animals together and organizing a search.

Tardy the tortoise and Dozy the dormouse were not well adapted for any kind of searching. One was too slow and the other too sleepy. So, while this frantic activity was going on, they sat outside the Obvious Cottage, having a philosophical discussion. "Why do they call you a tortoise?" asked Tardy sleepily. "Because I used to be an educator," he replied, without cracking a smile. Tortoises don't smile much, having little to smile about. "Why do they call you a dormouse?" It comes from the French, said the dormouse proudly. "In France I would be called *Le*

Loir." How do you get from *Le Loir* to Dormouse?" asked the Tortoise, irritably. "I've no idea," said the Dormouse, yawning. "It's a confusing language."

"What we need around here is a bit of education," the tortoise pronounced, suddenly more interested. "Look at all these animals, most of them quite illiterate. Mole writes up a lovely menu every day in his Bistro and they don't even look at it, they just eat."

"There's not much to read around here," said the Dormouse, "And in any case reading sends me to sleep. Now that Toad's library is gone, and Badger doesn't get anything new from the outside, there's nothing to read but Rat's poetry and Mole's menus. Pegasus said that animals don't need much more than instinct and common sense, and I think he's right. I think we learn by hearing stories, like this."

The Dormouse launched into a story about three girls who lived in a well and had nothing to eat but treacle. The Tortoise stopped him almost at once.

"Enough of that!" he cried, "We all know that story, and it's just silliness."

The Dormouse sulked for a while and soon drifted off to sleep, while the Tortoise thought about all the wonderful things he could teach these animals if only they would pay attention for more than a few seconds. He sighed.

The hunt for little Wally the Weasel spread out over the countryside. Maggie Magpie had volunteered again to lead the way from above, since she had flown over the territory of the Monsters before. The Old Goat came, along with Pegasus as liaison, and all the squirrels. The Stoats and Weasels joined in of course, including the binary newspaper reporters. The rabbits were left behind on the grounds that they would only get lost and cause confusion, the mice were too small for the job, and Toad himself refused to stir. But it was a formidable search party, and they were able to follow the tracks that Wally had left on the soft ground.

Little Wally was oblivious to all the uproar his disappearance had caused. He had been having a thoroughly good time. He had found the Monsters without difficulty because he knew the direction, and also because they were very large and made strange noises. The young and fearless newspaper reporter (in embryo) first tried to interview two giraffes, who towered above him like giant trees. Once he had got their attention, which wasn't easy, they politely bent their long necks down to the ground and enquired what he wanted to ask. Unfortunately, Wally had no idea what he wanted to ask. What do you ask a giraffe? Also he had forgotten to bring a notebook to go with his pencil. He thanked them and scurried off in search of a more accessible monster, closer to the ground.

The giraffes looked at one another in puzzlement. "What was that?" asked one. "Whatever it was it was very small," said the other. "It must be one of those miniature animals we've heard about, but it seemed harmless. Why do you think it had a pencil?" This was one of the many questions that crop up in the life of any giraffe and that was destined to go unanswered.

After wandering around for a while and seeing many monsters far too tall for him to talk to, Wally came to a riverbank on which rested a huge creature lying flat on the ground in the mud, apparently asleep. As long as he stayed lying down, Wally thought that he might get his attention and talk to him and so he crept up, whispered a greeting and an introduction into one enormous ear and, getting no response, asked: "So what is it like to be a...." and, having no idea what the creature was, came to an embarrassing stop.

The hippopotamus had heard this too many times in the zoo to trouble himself with a reply. Everybody, it seemed, wanted to know what it was like to be a hippopotamus but very few could pronounce the word. The fact of the matter was that it was very boring to be a hippopotamus, whether you could pronounce it or not. So, it was better, in his opinion, to pretend to be asleep, which he did.

The search party spotted them at that moment, as Little Wally was trying to talk to the Hippo on his mudbank. The bold squirrels didn't hesitate but, thinking that Wally was about to be eaten and hoping to save their friend by staging a distraction, they launched themselves from an overhanging tree onto the Hippo's head. He opened one eye, muttered "More Squirrels" in a disgusted tone, and closed his eye again.

Little Wally was quickly rescued, not that he needed or wanted to be rescued, and carried home protesting about the liberty of weasels and the freedom of the press. He was returned to his mother who told him in no uncertain terms how unwise it was to be a journalist, and even more unwise to go interviewing strange monsters, and she confiscated his pencil. These are the predictable slings and arrows of a young journalist's life, and Wally went on to be a famous foreign correspondent.

"You see," said the Dormouse, briefly woken by all the fuss, "That's what happens when animals get a taste for literacy. He's lucky he wasn't eaten."

"Phooey," said the tortoise. "Not everybody who can reads gets the notion of being an ace reporter. But perhaps it might be safer to start by teaching them some arithmetic."

"I know some arithmetic," said the Dormouse, eagerly. "If a dormouse wakes up and counts twenty million twinkling stars, and it's always six o'clock on Tuesday, and there's nothing but treacle for breakfast, how many slices of toast....?"

This time it was the turn of the tortoise to pull his head into his shell and go to sleep.

Chapter 13: The Accidental Astronaut

Toad had been brooding a lot recently, with a faraway look in his glaucous eyes that made Slimena anxious. His long convalescence after the fiery crash of the Toadmobile, and the destruction of Toad Hall had given him more than enough time to brood. He missed his fine house, and the Amphibian's Club where he could sit around and do nothing with his friends. He needed a new adventure, and this was going to be a big one. For a Toad of his quality, he felt, there was nowhere to go but up.

Toad had never been much of a reader but, before he burned down his own library, he had been fond of sensational adventure stories, and saw himself as the hero of them all. Some of these books he had rescued from the ruins, including science fiction novels by Jules Verne and HG Wells which described adventures not on this boring slow-moving earth but out there in space where everything seemed to go zoom, there were no speed limits, and anything was possible in Toad's fevered imagination. He had read that things weighed nothing in space. If this applied to Toads it would also be of great benefit to his expanding waistline.

So he gazed longingly at the pale moon floating in the daytime sky. Sometimes she seemed very close, surely not too far for a bold Toad to reach. After all he had driven all the way into the next county in one of his stolen cars. The heroes of his books had traveled to the moon without much trouble at all and had had many exciting adventures there. The mice might believe that the moon was made of green cheese, but this was nothing but wishful thinking.

Toad had been working on this idea for a long time and had engaged both teams of rats in his enterprise. The lab rats, who worked over in the obvious cottage, were given the most difficult task. In this annoying new world there was no motor fuel, or anything like it, to power a space machine. So he had set the lab rats the challenge of discovering a new kind of fuel that they could concoct from available ingredients. They had been bored and adopted this project with enthusiasm, starting as always with their favorite ingredient, garbage. They mixed garbage with various chemicals, vegetables, and odd unidentifiable things they found along the Riverbank, and tested the combustible qualities of each mixture. It was these experiments that had given rise to some small explosions in the obvious cottage, and complaints from his other inhabitants, especially Mole. But now, after much random experimentation and a few minor injuries, they had found a mixture that seemed to work. The chemical formula was garbage+something else+something orange+something slippery. They called it Ratolene, a substance that burned furiously with an awful smell when ignited but did not actually explode.

Meanwhile, on the other side of the river, the team of Dirty Rats who lived in the basement of the former Toad Hall had been collecting the necessary material to build Toad's spaceship. He had shown them illustrations from his books, and it looked simple enough: simply a tube with some kind of cabin or cockpit attached to the top, and enough Ratolene inside to send it on its way to the sky like a giant Guy Fawkes Day firework. Thus, while the lab rats had invented the first solid fuel ever seen in the New Wide World, the dirty rats were about to create the first space rocket. It was just as well that there were no greedy humans around. They who would certainly have claimed credit for everything.

The biggest problem for the Dirty Rats was the body of the rocket, which had to be strong, hollow, and large enough to hold plenty of fuel. One of them remembered the Toad's old steamship, the Viking, which he had wrecked further down the river long ago and which had blown up when the steam pressure was not turned off. There was a good chance that the wreckage was still lying on the bank, and part of it would be the funnel, a big metal tube that would be ideal for the body of a rocket. After some negotiation they persuaded Pegasus, sworn to secrecy, to take a cart down the towpath and, with great difficulty, they loaded the old funnel onto the cart and brought it back to their workshop in the stables behind the ruins of Toad Hall. Now the elements were all in place and work on Toad's spaceship went ahead much faster. The vessel was named the Toadship Enterprise, and this was painted along both sides.

As always Toad wanted to squeeze the maximum drama out of his voyage to outer space. But there were several cancellations because of technical problems or because the moon could not be seen and was therefore thought to have moved somewhere else. Not the least problem was that the rocket, when filled with Ratolene and topped off with a capsule for Toad, made out of a large dustbin, was too heavy to lift into the vertical position. Only the providential help of a couple of elephants, who had wandered over to see what was going on, allowed them to haul the heavy tube up. Then they had to let it down again because Toad had forgotten to get into the capsule first. Then the elephants good humoredly pulled it up again, and all was ready.

This was only the second time, after Water Rat's encounter with the Medical Bear, that the Riverbankers and those they still called The Monsters had cooperated It would not be the last.

"How many more times will Toad do crazy things like this this?" wondered the Mole. "He's not immortal and he must know that everybody comes just to see a disaster."

Both teams of rats were anxious. The Lab Rats had calculated that their Ratolene fuel would take the rocket all the way to infinity, or even slightly further, without slowing down, which could pose problems for the return journey. The Dirty Rats expected that it would just blow up and put their paws over their ears.

Slimena had the honor of lighting the blue touch paper at the base of the rocket, which she did when Toad waved a green flag out of the window. Then she hopped away as fast and as far as possible.

There was a hissing sound, a horrible smell, and the Starship Toad wobbled for a moment and began rising slowly, slowly into this sky on a column of smoke and flame. Everybody cheered except for Badger who said, sadly: "This madness will be the end of Toad," and walked heavily away.

Inside the capsule toad was seated in an old armchair, tied firmly in place with a piece of strong string, wearing a space suit designed by Slimena to protect him against what she imagined to be chilly conditions on the moon, and surrounded by food supplies. He couldn't see the moon from this position, but expected to see it when he got closer. When the fuel was ignited, the Toadship Enterprise shuddered for a moment, and began to rise very slowly from the ground, then faster and faster on a column of flame. Toad found himself flattened into his armchair until he was half his usual size. He had never encountered such a weight of gravity before. Toad's rocket was a remarkable achievement, but it was unfortunate that it had been constructed without any knowledge whatsoever of engineering, physics, astronomy, or even ordinary terrestrial common sense.

There were many things that Toad had not thought about in planning this space voyage: how to steer the rocket, how to land, how to refuel without the help of the rats, and how to take off on his return journey when he was at one end of the rocket and the blue touch paper was at the other. He had been carried away, as always, by a fantasy of power and speed without worrying about the details. So there was nothing to be done but endure this ferocious acceleration until it stopped. He hoped it would stop when they were in orbit, although he had no idea what that meant. As it turned out, none of this mattered.

For the spectators on the ground it was a spectacular sight. The Toadship Enterprise hurtled into the sky at an unbelievable speed and seemed likely to vanish into the stratosphere quite soon. The Laboratory Rats had claimed that the fuel they had provided would propel Toad all the way across the universe. But they had miscalculated by several thousand percent, and the fuel ran out after only two minutes. Toad, in the capsule, felt it. The roar of the rocket stopped abruptly, and the whole awkward contraption tilted and began heading down, straight down, quite unlike the slow glide of the airplane that toad had flown into the ground before. The rocket fell like a stone. Toad screamed and looked at the rapidly-approaching earth. There was no friendly pond or river waiting for him but only the solid ground. The rocket was spinning now, the lid of the capsule popped open and Toad fell out into the rushing air. His space suit billowed out like an inadequate parachute and, although Toad was still falling very fast, the rocket was falling faster. He could see it below getting closer and closer to the hard ground and knew he would be down there himself in a few seconds.

There seemed to be no hope for Toad until he felt himself seized from behind by the collar of his space suit, and the speed of his fall slowed abruptly. There was a great beating of wings, and Toad was conscious of a huge creature above him. But he was too scared for any ornithological reflections as he was brought down in a slow glide to earth and dropped, none too gently, on the ground in front of the astonished spectators. The Eagle looked around at the group and said severely: "You really should take better care of this fellow. Toads are not intended to fly. He's lucky I just happened to be passing, or there would be at toad shaped hole in the ground."

So saying the Eagle spread his great wings and disappeared into the sky. "I knew there were some big birds over there," chirped an awestruck sparrow, "But nothing that big." The Toadship Enterprise had crashed and exploded some distance away with a bang and a terrible smell, but all attention focused on the unfortunate amphibian lying on the ground, dazed, squashed, and thoroughly traumatized. Pegasus brought a cart, and the accidental astronaut was carried back to the old castle to be looked after, without too much sympathy, by Slimena and Ms Tiggywinkle. It was a humiliating end to Toad's venture into space and one which, out of kindness and delicacy, the other animals (apart from Slimena) never mentioned to him again.

Chapter fourteen: Amphibians on the Move

One of the favorite memories of those who lived in the Wild Wood and along the Riverbank was of the day when they had all gone to the seaside. Pegasus had pulled a cart full of animals all the way along the towpath until they had reached the ocean, where they spent a delightful day observing the antics of the human creatures enjoying their "holidays" at the beach. It was such a strange sight that they had never forgotten it and everyone, especially the younger animals who had missed the treat constantly pestered Pegasus to make the journey again although now, of course, there were no clownish human creatures to entertain them.

This summer Pegsus relented, even though the excursion would be hard work for him. He loved all the animals, and had been rather bored, since the convalescent Toad had had no jobs for him. There was some talk of making the excursion a regular event, even every weekend. But, as there were no weekends along the Riverbank, because there were no weekdays, this was a step too far for Pegasus. He was a sensible horse and not as young as he used to be. He firmly refused to make any commitment beyond this one trip.

The coach they had used before was still behind Toad Hall, in the stables that had been untouched by the fire. It was a long, narrow carriage with seats down the sides, which had had probably once been a horse omnibus, and it was ideal for the job. A willing crew of volunteers soon cleaned it and even touched up the gaudy paintwork.

The trip to the seaside was all they had expected, and more. The animals playing on the beach and on the edge of the sea exceeded in silliness even the human beings who had been there before, and they rode home exhausted and exhilarated with Pegasus wearily pulling the overloaded cart, but perfectly satisfied with the event.

As they got close to home Pegasus gazed reflectively over the water at the old barge. This was a piece of Riverbank history. When Toad had blown up his own steam yacht, the Viking, and left all the passengers stranded half way down the river, it was the barge pulled by Pegasus that had rescued them. Toad had been shamed into paying for the trip back home and had actually bought the barge itself for an extravagant price. There it sat in the river, alongside the ruins of Toad Hall, slowly rusting and sinking.

Pegasus thought this was a shame. It had been a fine, big barge, and he thought they should find a use for it. He was thinking, surprisingly, of Toad, who had been having a very bad time recently. His two most recent adventures had been embarrassing and painful disasters, he had lost his fine home, and he had lost the Amphibian club which had been his delight. Ms. Tiggywinkle refused to have the club in the old castle, which she thought was wet enough already, and there was nowhere else for the amphibians to go.

Pegasus's ingenious idea was to restore the barge as a new home for The Amphibian's Club. It would give Toad an occupation, and some of his dignity back, and it might stop the other amphibians from trying to slither into dryer and more traditional clubs, where they were just a nuisance. The location on the river was ideal, and a simple structure on top of the barge would suffice because all the amphibians ever did was to sit around with their friends and do nothing. They didn't even care if it rained on them

Slimena was consulted secretly, and thought it was a brilliant idea. Not only would it get Toad and his idle friends out of the Castle during the day, but the barge might sink, sooner or later. Sooner, she hoped.

At the first opportunity Pegasus clip-clopped up the hill to see the Oracat and ask what he thought of the plan. "It's a brilliant idea," said the Oracat "And it will end in disaster." This was not a very original prediction because every project involving Toad ended in disaster. Pegasus turned politely to the Orakitten with the same question. "I don't know anything about old barges," she said disdainfully. "But I can tell you this. Toad will eventually learn to love Slimena, but not half as much as he loves himself."

Pegasus clip clopped back down the hill again reflecting that a visit to the prophetic cats was never worth the time and energy. But, like a visit to the vet, it was oddly reassuring. You asked your questions and got your answers. The answers could be quickly forgotten. Asking was the important thing.

It was the beginning of summer and Pegasus wasted no time. On the way home his visited the Beavers in the old castle. Construction skills would be required for this job and, for most of the animals, making a nest out of old newspapers was the limit of their skills. The barge was ready-made, and sturdy. All it needed was a simple structure on top to accommodate the club.

The Beavers had also been bored in this quiet time. Their weekly routine of building a dam, flooding the castle, and watching Ms Tiggywinkle clean it out, had become tedious. It also made them slightly guilty about giving her all that work, although Beavers are not much given to guilt when it comes to floods. They listened attentively to Pegasus and looked at the diagram he scratched in the mud with his front hoof.

"We're busy," they said, "But we might find time for this."

When the Beavers got going, they were astonishingly efficient. Heaps of wood were floated down the river and trimmed to size. Some old beams from the wreckage of the Hall made a sturdy framework, and the walls and roof were filled in using the same clever weaving technique that the Beavers used for their dams. Not much furniture was required, but plenty of chairs and couches were available from the vast junk room of the Obvious Cottage.

The New Amphibian Club was long and low, and had a decidedly rustic appearance, but Toad was enraptured by it. Over the door was painted: "The New Amphibian Club: Director, Permanent Secretary, Master of Ceremonies and Chief of Protocol: The Right Honorable Mr. Toad." He almost added Ms Tiggywinkle's name underneath, in much smaller letters, for she was again taking on the management of the enterprise. But he was afraid that excessive flattery would turn her prickly head.

The Club was an instant success. All the old members came slithering back along with some new ones from the world outside. It was the ideal club for male animals. They all sat around and did nothing, and occasionally Toad made a speech or sang a song in praise of himself, to a background of heavy snoring. Nothing in the least interesting happened until well into the summer, when a newt, waking up briefly and looking out of the window, noticed that the scenery was moving past. The whole Club was drifting downriver on the current! A remarkable amount of panic ensued, considering that they were all amphibians. Toad himself didn't help with his shrieks of "We're all doomed!" and the sensible Ms Tiggywinkle had to take over.

"Don't panic! There is a bend in the river just ahead," she announced loudly. "This big barge will never get around the bend. We will run aground, and you can all get safely home without getting your feet or your flippers wet. Anyway, you can all swim." Almost as soon as she said this, the barge reached the bend in the river and gently ran aground in the mud. There was a great sigh of relief all around the club, and the members scrambled out on deck to see where they were and how long it might take to get back. Unfortunately, they had company, refugees from the old zoo. Several huge green creatures lay basking in the mud around the grounded barge. They smiled at the stranded club members showing rows of sharp teeth and made ironic comments about amphibians who should never go near the water. But they didn't offer to help. The amphibians retreated inside their club and waited to be rescued.

Help was not long in coming. Everyone had seen the barge drifting away, and the more intelligent observers had realized that it would never drift as far as the sea but would get stuck on one of the sharp bends in the river, probably the first one they came to. Pulling the barge back would be a strenuous task, and Pegasus decided to ask for help from some new friends he had made in the neighborhood outside the hedge horses who had worked on farms, or sometimes on racecourses, or sometimes in stables where they would carry little girls around and jump over artificial obstacles. They all knew Pegasus by this time, and admired him, and two of the farm horses were more than willing to accompany him down the towpath to the stranded barge. The zoo alligators had been told to go away but they hung around and made ironic comments as the horses struggled to pull the barge out of the mud but did nothing to help. A few hours later the barge was back in place securely tied to its mooring bollards by some exceptionally thick rope.

It was a mystery how this accident to the barge had happened, but not for long. Water Rat, Otter and Not So Little Portly formed an investigating team and examined the evidence. They considered a lightning strike (but there was no storm), a tidal wave (same problem), and a sudden collapse of one of the beaver dams releasing a flood of water (which the Beavers hotly denied). Somebody suggested that the barge had been struck and torn from its moorings by a passing whale. This was dismissed as very silly, but time would show that it was not as silly as they thought.

The only solid evidence was the mooring rope of the barge, which showed signs of having been nibbled through by sharp little teeth. Water Rat decided that this was conclusive. "When you have eliminated the ridiculous," he said, "Whatever remains, however preposterous, must be the truth." This conclusion pointed straight to the Little Bunnies, who were notorious for their foolish pranks. They soon confessed and apologized. It was just a joke, they said. They had thought that the barge would drift a little way from the bank and the club members would have to jump into the water to get ashore, which the bunnies thought would be very entertaining. They never imagined that the barge would sail away like that...and so on and so on. The Little Bunnies were duly admonished by Water Rat and deprived of carrots for a week.

The Amphibian Club resumed its usual round completely useless inactivities, and Toad was able to feel a person of importance again. His greatest triumph came when a bedraggled old toad arrived at the door and was granted an audience with Toad himself. He proved to be none other than the notorious Lord Slimy Toad, once the greatest toad in the county, who had been driven into retirement in a remote pond by the revelation of that he was not who he pretended to be. He had come now to humbly crave admission to the Amphibian Club. Lady Slimy Toad was long gone, and his lordship was lonely. Toad made a long and slippery speech about toad ethics, and finally agreed to admit Lord slimy toad to the club on the condition that he dropped the "Lord" from his title and became just Slimy Toad. After that, the sight of the old villain in a corner armchair invariably gave Toad immense satisfaction.

Pegasus too was rather proud of himself for rescuing the barge and making some useful new friends. The little bunnies were chastened, but not for long and not so chastened as to prevent them from sneaking around the back of Mole's Bistro and stealing the forbidden carrots.

Chapter fifteen: A Visit to the Monsters

The Water Rat was doing what he liked best, rowing gently down the river on a warm summer's day with his friend the Mole. Strictly speaking, he didn't need to row, because he had mastered the art of sailing. After his disastrous adventure, when he sailed out of the river and into the ocean without being able to control his little boat, he had studied the subject and consulted with the birds who knew all about winds and how to use them. Now his rowing boat had a small mast and a triangular sail which he could use when he needed it, especially when coming back upstream against the tide. He could tack from side to side and make progress even when the wind was against him, and he was very proud of this new skill.

However, such is the obstinacy of water rat nature, that he preferred to row as he was doing now and had always done. It was soothing, and the sound of the oars dipping and splashing was the most reassuring sound he knew.

"It doesn't get much better than this Ratty," said Mole, lounging on the stern seat on a couple of cushions.

"Everything seems to be back to normal, more or less."

"I'm not so sure," said Water Rat seriously. "We still need to come to terms with these new creatures all around us, and we know so little about them. We met one or two, and they were very agreeable. The medical Bear dressed my paw for example, and it's fine now." He looked at his paw which was indeed as good as new. "And those elephants were helpful with Toad's stupid rocket. But how do we get to know them better when we are so small and some of them are so big and so different from us?"

Mole had no answer, so he closed his eyes and snoozed for a while, only to be woken by an excited quacking of ducks. Opening his eyes, he saw that it was their friends the Mallards, who were urgently trying to tell the Water Rat something. It was hard to hear what, because they were all quacking at once, but it seemed that they had been startled a little further down the river by the sight of a gigantic fish, bigger than anything they had ever seen before, that jumped and plunged and spouted water from the top of its head. It must have come in from the sea, they said, because the river fish were so small and modest that you scarcely even noticed them.

The river estuary, where it ran into the sea, had become a sort of meeting and greeting place for the freshwater and the saltwater creatures, and a neutral zone between the two animal worlds. Otter now had friends among the sea otters and the mallard ducks maintained at least a nodding acquaintance with the sea ducks, who led very different lives.

"It must be a whale," said the Mole. "I have read about whales, they live in the ocean, and they are supposed to be enormous, so maybe one of them has found his way into our River. This is very exciting."

The ducks were not so much excited as alarmed. Nobody expects whales in a quiet English river. They wanted to know what or who this whale was going to eat. It took a little while for Water Rat to calm them down and to reassure them that it might be some kind of mistake and that in any case if the fish was that big they would soon be able to find it and see if it was going to be any kind of problem.

It was not clear who was best qualified to go searching for this supposed whale until Captain Duck appeared. He was a beautiful pure white Peking duck, called "Captain" by courtesy because he was larger than the mallards and bolder than any of them. He had come from a farm at the time of the great change, when all farm animals were liberated, and had found himself very welcome and comfortable on the river.

"I don't see the problem here," said the Captain, who assumed that whales, like any other animals in this new world, must be domesticated and friendly. "I'll just paddle up the river as far as I can and see if I can locate this whale and have a word with him. Then I will come back and tell you fellows all about it."

At this moment, and suspiciously on cue, the Water Rat's little boat gave a violent lurch and almost turned over, as if something had struck it from under the water. Before the animals had recovered their wits a broad friendly face surfaced alongside the boat and smiled apologetically. "Sorry about that, clumsy of me," it said, still smiling. I was just trying to get a better look at you fellows because I've never seen you before. Are you some kind of fish?"

"No, of course not," said the Rat, still startled by this sudden appearance. "Are you some kind of whale?"

"No, no, said the cheerful creature I'm some kind of dolphin, much smaller than a whale, although we are related, of course." And they could see now that this new acquaintance, although very much bigger than any fish in the river, was not remotely as big as the whales they had imagined. In fact he was only a little longer than Water Rats rowing boat, and a beautiful shiny gray in color, with a long elegant nose and a winning smile showing a lot of teeth.

"We thought you were a whale," explained Water Rat. "Captain White Duck here was just going to look for you." The dolphin frowned. "I think your storyline has got a bit confused," he said at last "But never mind, it's all clear now."

When the introductions had been completed, and Water Rat had explained the purpose of the boat, which the dolphin found very puzzling (why, he wondered, would you want to go around on top of the water when you could be in it), they began to chat about things in general. Water Rat was eager to question this obviously intelligent animal about the relationship between the Wildwood and the Riverbank and all their new neighbors who had come, like the dolphin, from the vanished zoo.

The dolphin understood the problem immediately. "We are much too big and clumsy to come and visit you," he said. "But you could come and get to know us. That splendid horse Pegasus has already been over to discuss some details about boundaries, and there was that very funny scene when your squirrels rescued one of your little guys from the hippo," and the dolphin laughed so hard that he choked and shot a fountain of water out of his blowhole, soaking everybody.

When things had settled down the dolphin had a serious suggestion. "It's quite a long way to walk from your Wild Wood to where we are, but it's easy to get there by water," he explained. "There's a tributary that runs from beside the old castle right up to where the zoo used to be. You could come and visit, and be back in a day. You would be very welcome."

It was an invitation impossible to refuse and, a couple of days later when arrangements had been made for the invaluable Ms Tiggywinkle to look after Bistro Mole, our two heroes set out to meet the monsters. They quickly found the tributary that the Dolphin had mentioned – in fact it was the same one that the Beavers were in the habit of blocking with their dams, but they reluctantly agreed to take a break, just for today. And so began one of the most memorable days that the two friends had ever spent.

The winding tributary led them through beautiful countryside, with flowering meadows and green woods on every side, and a riotous growth of reeds and water lilies along the banks that tangled Water Rat's oars, and small river bank creatures who popped out to see what was going on and complain about the disturbance. It was not really a great distance, but he was tired and relieved when they emerged quite suddenly into a broad lake filled with animals and birds. The variety of sights and sounds was extraordinary, and Water Rat just let his boat drift while they gazed at the pink flamingoes, more varieties of ducks than they knew existed, and even a crowd of penguins waiting impatiently for winter. On the shore lay several hippos and alligators, and gazelles had come down to drink.

"Oh my, oh my," exclaimed Mole. "The world really must be a very big place if it has all these creatures in it.'

They drifted on the lake for a while, amazed, until they were surrounded by a school of playful dolphins who escorted them to the shore, where they found they had a guide – none other than the Medical Bear who had helped Water Rat a short time ago. He examined Rat's paw briefly and beamed at them.

"We're very glad you came," he said, "And since we have met already I have volunteered to give you the Grand Tour of our little animal community. Don't expect too much. The animals have been spreading out across the country since the zoo vanished, so some of them are missing, and you won't want to walk too far on those little, short legs of yours." This was a bit cheeky, coming from a bear who was decidedly rotund and had rather short legs himself. He became conscious of this and hurried on." We'll meet the animals who have stayed close to the lake. Some of them are rather shy and not very talkative, and please don't stare at them – they got tired of being stared at in the zoo. Off we go."

The Medical Bear lumbered off, followed by Water Rat and Mole, who could scarcely believe what was happening.

They stopped first by a small herd of Zebras, whose black and white stripes made our heroes stare in spite of themselves. The Zebras were used to this and explained that they had been originally designed for a planet where the vegetation was all black and white, and then accidentally dropped by the exterior decorating mice on this one where everything was brown and green. They had not entirely forgiven the mice for this carelessness, and neither had the pandas.

The small sightseers also stared up in awe at the giraffes, who graciously bent their long necks down to say hello, and at dozens of animals large and small, most of whom were willing to pass the time of day. Some, like Wombats, Armadillos and Platypuses, were not terribly big but looked very strange and had peculiar accents. The visitors were most impressed and scared by the big cats, who padded by silently on errands of their own, but without presenting the slightest threat.

Mole whispered: "Do you remember one of the Old Goat's stories, where the big animals were just like this? Perhaps it was true." Rat thought it might be true and wondered what it meant. But the guiding bear kept them moving briskly from group to group, and there wasn't much time for speculation.

There was a brief delay when a playful young elephant picked up Water Rat with his trunk in order to get a closer look at him, but set him down on his feet again with apologies when the bear pointed out that this was no way to treat a visitor.

They were passing through a small wood when there was a rustle of leaves from above and a huge snake uncoiled and hung from one of the branches right over their heads. Water Rat jumped backwards, and Mole screamed and fell flat on his face.

"Isn't that just typical?" said the snake, bitterly. "Why am I scarier than the other animals? We haven't even been introduced. It's blatant discrimination."

"But you're a snake," Mole quavered.

"Oh, I know, I know, it's that old story again. Somewhere back in the beginning of time a relative of mine was hanging out in a tree just like this when a new kind of female creature came along. It was a hot day, and she had shed all her fur. She told him that she was hungry, and so my ancestor offered her an apple from his tree, which she took without a word of thanks. And, can you believe it? the human creatures (for that's what she was, an early example of the human creatures) made a whole religion out of me and that apple and spent thousands of years killing and torturing one another because of it, so that even now everybody is afraid of snakes. Does that make any sense to you?" the snake concluded bitterly.

Mole ventured the opinion that human creatures had been strange. "Strange like the devil is strange," the serpent grumbled. "I met him once, you know, the devil. Charming fellow, wonderful sense of humor. Perhaps those humans were an example of it. But the white mice got rid of them at last."

They agreed that it was all very sad, and made sympathetic noises, but the snake was not to be comforted. He coiled himself back up into his tree after offering them each an apple, which they politely declined, and left him to his theological refections.

The sun was getting low in the sky when they returned to the lake and thanked the Medical Bear for a most amazing day. "You're very welcome, come back any time" he laughed, "Stay healthy. I recommend an apple a day," and he pushed the little boat out into the water for its return journey.

Everyone except Toad wanted to know about the Monsters. Toad had been scared to go but boasted that he would launch a much bigger and braver expedition later, which he never did. The heroes of the day, Ratty and Mole, were even asked to give a lecture about it, and Water Rat was on fire to get everything he had seen down on paper in paintings or poems, or paintings about poems, or poems about paintings. For months this was his passion and, eventually, their whole travel experience was laid out in an exhibition in the Obvious Cottage simply called "The Monsters." Nobody really believed what they saw, but the show was enormously popular.

"We can't ignore these new neighbors, with only a fragile hedge between us. We must be friends," said Badger firmly. And, once Badger had spoken, the matter was settled.

Chapter sixteen: Toad's Memoir

The friendship between the two communities grew, as it will between good neighbors – not too close, not too distant, but always companionable. Groups of

Riverbank and Wild Wood animals, chaperoned by Pegasus in the small cart, paid visits to the Monsters outside the wall. The former zoo animals were very particular about privacy, but their curiosity brought them to Water Rat's hedge where they peered through (or in the case of the giraffes over) the foliage to see how the little creatures lived on the Wild Wood side. Most of the time, especially when winter came on, it was a rather unexciting spectacle (a lot of eating, a lot of sleeping). But it was a novelty, and every Monster loves a novelty. They also developed an almost paternalistic concern for the small creatures. As the Eagle remarked, "They seem to need rescuing a lot," and this was true enough.

However, as is always the case, more was happening than appeared on the grassy surface. Cooler evenings meant more time spent in the Obvious Cottage or in Badger's comfortable sett. There had been a lot to talk about this year, and talking was one of the things the friends did best.

"Perhaps we shouldn't live so much in the past," suggested Water Rat one evening, when they were lazily retelling their favorite stories. We are going to live in the future, not the past, so maybe we should think about that and make some plans."

"How can we live in the future when it's not here yet," asked Mole, irritably. "The only place we can possibly live is in the present, and it's the best place to be, especially around lunchtime. I learned to focus on the present from Ms Tiggywinkle, who knows a lot of philosophy. She calls it 'Mindfulness. She says that, as long as everything is going to happen again, we might as well stay when we are and just wait for it."

Water Rat rubbed his head and blinked a few times. "I'm not sure I understand that," he said. "We need the Oracat to sort this out. He lives in the future all the time."

"But it's an *imaginary* future, cried the exasperated Mole. "The Cat just makes it all up, and the Kitten is worse."

Badger intervened at this point, to prevent the argument from getting heated.

"You're forgetting," he said gravely, "How very easy and pleasant it is to live in the past. It's like reading a book you have already read. Everything that will happen has happened, there are no surprises, and you can always go back and read it again, and it will be exactly the same."

This silenced the discussion for a moment. Pegasus was not present at this meeting, or he might have sided with the Water Rat, Ms Tiggywinkle herself was busy in the Castle, and Tardy the Tortoise, the only other animal (or reptile) who could possibly be considered an intellectual was in a remote corner of the Obvious Cottage that he had designated The Unseen University. Professor Tardy, the only member of the so far nonexistent faculty, was instructing a small class of torpid creatures on the inspirational subject of Einstein in Slow Motion. Dozy the Dormouse, who was dreaming at the back of the class, was widely expected to graduate with honors.

But there was a surprise in store. Sally Stoat alias Emilie Ermine, the newspaper reporter, had arrived in just in time to hear Badger's last remarks. She/they at once joined the discussion, announcing with pride: "If it's history and nostalgia you want, we have the past all wrapped up for you. Toad's Memoir is finished." This caused a sensation. Few animals believed that this memoir had ever existed, and those who did never believed that it would be finished. But here it was, a plump volume bound with cardboard (leather would obviously have been in bad taste) and printed on the antique machine normally used to produce *The Riverbank Record.* The journalists did not anticipate strong sales and had settled on an initial print run of one copy.

The Riverbank community, frankly, was a bit of a literary desert. There was no bookstore or library. Books were quite rare and were treated with excessive reverence because they were thought to contain nothing but the truth. This naïve belief did not survive the appearance of Toad's memoir.

The Title on the cardboard cover was: "The Astonishing Life and History of Mr. Toad, formerly of Toad Hall, by Emilia Ermine and Sally Stoat." At the bottom of the cover, in very small letters, were the words: "With occasional suggestions from Mr. Toad."

"Will this make us all famous?" asked Mole, breathlessly.

"Not if there is only one copy," Badger replied. "But it might make us all look ridiculous."

The two authors proposed a Launch Party the following day, which Mole promptly decided must be a Lunch Party, and everyone was invited (although they forgot to invite Toad himself until the last minute). In fact, the authors had some doubts about how Toad would react, when and if he read the book.

In the event Toad had multiple reactions, starting with delight and ending with rage. He was enormously excited to know that the book was finished, and immediately decided that it would make him famous and so rich that he could rebuild Toad Hall. The book itself was something of a disappointment, with its cardboard cover and (to him) completely false description of authorship, even though Toad had never written a word of it himself, and the contents struck him as an outrage.

Toad had always thought of himself as a distinguished gentleman far above the other animals and amphibians and birds who lived around the Riverbank. He was, in his own mind, handsome, creative, adventurous and, in his sophisticated lifestyle, a model for every animal who came in contact with him. This so-called memoir with its devastating portrait of idiotic antics and childish enthusiasms, was not how he wanted to be seen at all.

Toad was already unhappy about being a mere lodger in the old castle. It was dark and chilly, even in summer, and he hated getting prickled every time he had to slide past Ms Tiggywinkle in one of the narrow corridors and tolerating the weekly floods unleashed by the busy Beavers. Now, on top of all that, was this humiliating memoir that described his glorious life only as a series of jokes and clownish disasters. In fact one of the longest chapters dwelt on the unhappy period when Toad had literally been made into a clown by a bunch of circus people. It really was too much. Toad longed to do something other than just being a toad, and he determined there and then to do something new and dazzling with his life. "I'm getting out of here," he announced to everyone. "I'm going to a place far away where I might be appreciated, and I'm not coming back."

This was assumed to be one of Toad's empty threats, especially as nobody now believed that he had really ventured outside the hedge to see the monsters. In his mind he saw monsters everywhere. He had been terrified by the sight of a rhinoceros walking past on the other side of the hedge, even though it had only said a polite "good morning." "It was as big as a house," Toad told Slimena, "And it made the earth shake. I'm not going out there." It seemed unlikely that the nervous Toad would venture on an adventurous journey to a far distant land.

Everybody wanted to read Toad's memoir, and those who couldn't read had it read aloud to them. It wasn't just Toad's memoir, it was everyone's memoir, and they all wanted to enjoy it. Such was the demand that

Sally and Emelia printed a second copy, and there was some speculation that it could become a great commercial success if only the publishing business still existed. As it happened, in spite of the modest scale of the journalists' book production, nobody was ever able to forget Toad of Toad Hall.

So, while Toad sulked in the castle, they ignored his outburst and paid no attention to the preparations he was making for his escape. Slimena, by contrast, *did* pay attention. She too was discontented and thoroughly bored in the claustrophobic and uncomfortable castle and irritated by the eternally cheerful Ms. Tiggywinkle and her incendiary dragon. The idea of being left there without Toad, no matter what a dismal companion he was, was something that Slimena did not want to contemplate. She was used to Toad in all his variable moods, and she remembered the wild ride they had taken long ago in the car that Toad had stolen from her father and how thrilling it had all been. She could see something of the same maniacal determination in Toad now and hoped that it might lead to something equally liberating or at least a change of scene. So, she started a charm offensive, which Toad failed to notice until she complimented him on his book. "You were so adventurous," she told him. "People will still be reading about the exploits of Mr. Toad of Toad Hall in a hundred years." Toad swelled up. In the old days, when he wore human clothes, he would have popped the buttons off his waistcoat. He began to think more kindly about Slimena who, after all, came from a distinguished family and had stuck by him through many adventures. They began to argue about plans together.

The Water Rat, meanwhile, had put into action *his* notion of planning for the future. Pegasus was an enthusiastic supporter, and especially useful because they needed to explore more territory in order to learn more about this new world. A group of farm animals, staying close to their old home, were a bit of a puzzle, being less articulate and sophisticated than the former zoo animals. Rat studied them and decided that, unlike most animals he knew, they all had a particular talent and purpose in life: chickens for eggs, cows for milk, and ducks and pigs for conversation. The friends talked constantly about all these things, trying to make sense of what had happened.

"Did we imagine those White Mice?' asked Mole, for the twentieth time. "If it was the Mice who did all this, they are like gods, although rather small and squeaky. "

"We all saw the mice," replied Badger. "It was strange, but we must admit that they were here, and they did what they did. Other animals may claim that White Mice are false gods and that the real gods are harvest mice, or perhaps shrews, or even Badgers. But once we start down that path, we will never find a way out."

Their theology was obviously a work in progress, but Badger was satisfied to leave things as they were. "If we carry on like this, without worrying about who did what and why, nothing can go wrong," he said. The Oracat kept quiet about his own feline philosophy, which was that nothing made any sense whatsoever, that they should enjoy this pleasant life as long as the tuna supply held out, and that it would all end in disaster.

But everything was going well for the moment. Once friendly relationships had been established across the Hedge, the inhabitants of the Wild Wood and the Riverbank (except Toad) had no hesitation about visiting their bigger neighbors, who looked down on them with a kind of bemused affection. They too wanted to learn more. One day the Medical Bear, sitting by the lake with Water Rat and Mole, while young rabbits were playing on the shore, leaned over and asked confidentially: "Tell me, if it's not rude to ask, what is the point of rabbits?" Water Rat couldn't come up with a sensible reply. Most of the farm animals seemed to have a point and a purpose, but not rabbits. He couldn't even decide what was the point of Water Rats. So he simply said "Diversity," which did not satisfy the bear at all.

Out of sight across the river, Toad was hard at work, or at least the Dirty Rats were hard at work. Toad had remembered that he did have a means of escape, not across the monster-infested land or even more perilously by air, but by water. The modest little steam motor launch that he had bought after he had exploded the beautiful yacht Viking had scarcely been used, and was tucked away in the boathouse which, like the stables, had escaped the fire. Toad had forgotten all about it in his enthusiasm for flying. There was nothing wrong with the little boat which had originally been named The Tadpole, but which was now renamed The Beagle after Darwin's famous exploration ship, except that she was dirty and dusty. There was no problem about fuel because the engine burned wood. So, the dirty rats, rather reluctantly, had been set to work once more on a cleanup job, on the promise of large quantities of cheese (although Toad planned to rat on his promise, as they should have known from past experience).

Once the little launch was ready, loaded with Toad food, wood chopped small by the Beavers, and matches to relight the boiler if necessary, Toad brought it out of the boathouse and paraded up and down the river, chuffing and tooting, at its maximum speed of about four miles an hour.

"Oh no!" cried Water Rat in horror, as he saw the smoking funnel passing above the reeds, "He's remembered the little steam, boat." But it was too late to do anything about it although, as with all Toad's manias, there was really nothing they could have done. Toad was really planning to sail away.

On the appointed departure day, as The Beagle was huffing away at her moorings ready to go, Toad made a little speech on the Riverbank.

"You fellows have searched far and wide – very brave and praiseworthy and all that – but you haven't found anything except fields and woods and dangerous animals. So, it seems to me that all the good places with roads and cars and no policemen and more sympathetic biographers must be on the other side of the big sea that the birds have told us about. The white mice can't have ruined the whole planet. We will make a new life in the land across the ocean. Goodbye."

The "we" was another surprise to the listeners. Nobody expected Slimena to go with him. But there she was, in a sailor's hat, on the deck of the launch, carrying a telescope, looking as beautiful as a young toad can look, which is not beautiful at all. Is it a kind of honeymoon trip? The animals wondered and got no answer.

Without waiting for any farewell speeches from the shore, which were not forthcoming, Toad set the little steamer in motion, Slimena waved regally at the group on shore, and the sound of their wrangling could be heard long after the boat had vanished downriver into the autumn mist.

Badger said (not for the first time): "I'm afraid that is the last we shall see of Toad."

Water Rat said: "They will never survive the open sea in that little boat. I know, I've been there. Toad knows nothing about the sea."

Mole said, almost tearfully: "Oh my, oh my, it's so sad, now they are gone forever."

They were all wrong, of course.

Chapter seventeen: The Clock

After Toad's indignant departure life on the Riverbank was peaceful, but not dull. The animals continued their usual round of autumn activities which mostly had to do with food and nesting. Occasionally they thought about the departed Toad and his unlikely companion, but his wild activities began to seem like a dream. Some of his old friends were even nostalgic. "He didn't even take his memoir," said Mole sadly. But the memoir, widely shared, kept memories alive, and the stories were inflated and exaggerated more and more as time went on, until Toad became an almost mythical figure.

The Water Rat was too practical a creature to indulge in such dreamy illusions. He had determined to spend this quiet time planning for the future of his little community by learning more about its past. Badger had advised him very seriously that you must understand the past before you can even think about the future. So, the methodical water rat had become a kind of explorer and archaeologist rolled into one. He traveled far and wide with Pegasus and interviewed the other animals they met. Closer to home, he searched for answers among the few remaining relics of the vanished Wide World that were still visible in the Obvious Cottage, the ruins of Toad Hall, and the Old Castle. All these proved to be rich in clues, but understanding them was another matter.

Water Rat collected all of his discoveries that were small enough to be moved in one of the empty rooms of the Obvious Cottage and invited everyone to stop by and make comments. Most visitors were baffled by the alien objects, but those who had had more contact with the human creatures in the old world could often put a name to the exhibits, and even explain how they had been used. The Rats, both clean and dirty, could sometimes identify the strangest things, and Edward and Henrietta, who had lived in a house a long time, were very good at explaining domestic objects. In this way Water Rat was able to build up a picture of the lives led by the vanished creatures, and sometimes even find a practical use for the objects they had left behind.

Some things needed no explanation. Furniture, although not much use to the animals, was obviously what it was. An old shotgun was recognized with horror by the rabbits, and Badger quickly had it thrown into the river. Kitchen utensils were equally obvious and found the home in the kitchen of Bistro Mole. But many of the discoveries were electrical, and therefore doubly mysterious. They knew what electricity was. They had seen the lights at Toad Hall, but Toad understood nothing about it and let his servants take care of everything electrical. They had amused themselves by plunging him into darkness from time to time and pretending that the rabbits were responsible. But there had never been any electricity along the Riverbank or in the Wild Wood, and they had never felt the need for it. Nor did they have any idea where to get it if it was needed.

The object that puzzled them the most, and that they never fully understood, was a heavy cylindrical thing with the tube at one end and a wire coming out of the other. Henrietta the hamster said she had seen it many times, in fact almost every day, but never knew what the humans thought that they were doing with it.

"It made a terrible noise," she said, covering her little ears as she remembered, "It was impossible to sleep, and they pushed it around the room for what seemed like hours. Perhaps it was meant to do something to the floor, but the floor never changed, it was always the same color." A messenger mouse was sent into the tube to explore, but came out, sneezing, to report that there was nothing up there but dust and dirt. So, they simply called it the noise machine and it remained an enigma.

Another very mysterious object was in two parts connected by a piece of wire, with another wire trailing out of the back. It was all black, and a very odd shape indeed. Edward and Henrietta had both seen people using this, and explained as best they could. "They would hold the small part of the thing to their face and talk to it, as if it was alive, like us. Sometimes they talked for a long time, but the machine never talked back, although they paused sometimes as if it was talking back. But that would mean that their voices were going along a piece of wire, which makes no sense at all. Henrietta thinks it may have been a device for having an imaginary conversation with other humans somewhere else, a sort of practice for when they actually met."

"Why have a complicated thing like this when you could send Messenger Mice?" asked the Water Rat. "Didn't they have any Messenger Mice?" It seemed that they had not, which seemed very strange to the other animals. Henrietta explained that the humans, especially the female ones, seemed to have an absolute horror of mice in the house, and were even afraid of them. Nobody believed this, especially not the mice.

The discovery that made the greatest impact was at first thought to be just another piece of useless furniture. But the animals who had been around humans recognized it at once. It was a tall wooden box with a white glass-covered circle at the top. "It's a clock," they exclaimed, and once again it was the task of Edward and Henrietta to explain what the awkward-looking thing was for.

"It measures time," said Edward, "They called it a clock. It tells you what time of the day it is."

"But we always know what time of day it is," said Mole, tapping his stomach. "It's breakfast time, lunchtime, or suppertime, or sometimes time for a snack."

"No, no," said Edward. "For the people it was very much more than that, it was a kind of mechanical organizer that controlled everything in their lives. The day was divided up into little slices, called minutes and hours, and at each hour and each minute on the clock they had to do some particular thing. They were always busy because of the clock, and they couldn't even sleep without a clock beside the bed to tell them when they should begin to be busy again. If they didn't have a clock they were afraid that they would waste some time."

This was something quite beyond the understanding of most of the animals. Their lives were divided by day and night and, as Mole had pointed out, by mealtimes. They couldn't imagine being harassed from sunrise to sunset by these artificial fractions of time. And what could it possibly mean to "waste time"? Now that they thought about it they remembered that Toad had had a clock like this at Toad Hall and was very proud of it. But he never looked at it, and indeed had never set it running, because Toad hated to be hurried. It was just another symbol of his wealth and importance.

But it was tempting to set this old clock running, if it would run. Several of the dirty rats, who loved a machine of any kind, clambered into the mechanism and explored it. Hanging together on one of the heavy weights they pulled it down, and then gave a shove to the pendulum. The clock went tick, then tock, then did it again, and it was running. With each tick and tock, the pointers at the top moved a fraction. They all watched it, hypnotized, heads going from side to side like spectators at a tennis match. But what did that mean? It was the turn of the Lab Rats to explain.

"Those numbers around the white circle are times," said the Chief Rat, pointing, and those two black arrow things tell you what time it is now. It is ten minutes to twelve."

"Almost lunchtime, observed Mole.

For some reason this discovery captured the imagination of many of the animals, especially the bunnies. They had never known what time it was before. Now they set about dividing their lives into hours and minutes, with tasks and activities for every part of the day – hopping along the Riverbank at nine, rolling on the grass at nine-thirty, diving into the burrow at ten-fifteen, and so on. They became fanatical about it, and soon began making timetables for everyone else too. Badger had a schedule for reading and thinking, Water Rat for rowing on the river and visiting the castle, and Mole found that every moment of his work at Bistro Mole was now rigidly fixed to a particular time. Ther lives became (if they had known it) like a speeded-up version of an old cartoon film, as they rushed in to see the clock and rushed out to do whatever the clock demanded. Nobody had thought to allocate ten or twelve hours for sleep, so they were all tired and red-eyed.

"For goodness' sake don't tell them about the calendar," whispered Badger to the Lab Rats. "They would have a date for everything." And it was Mr. Badger, his own eyes strained from too much reading, who finally declared that enough was enough, that time was a human idea and not at all suitable for animals. Everyone was exhausted by the effort if keeping up with it. Even the bunnies were flagging and falling behind on their daily list of tasks. By general consent, and to the relief of everyone, the clock was stopped.

Chapter eighteen: After the Fall

The fine, tall hedge that surrounded the territory of the Wild Wood and the Riverbank, now familiarly known as Ratty's Hedge, had only one entrance. It was quite small, so that the big zoo animals could not come through, but they never showed any signs of wanting to. The Hedge was seen as almost taboo. There was no gate at the entrance, no guard, and not even a sign saying, "Keep Out" or "Welcome." Badger said it was symbolic barrier, but mole argued that on the contrary it was just something that could be mistaken for something else but was not something else at all but another thing. They hoped that professor Tardy the academic tortoise would settle this dispute eventually.

But anyone small enough fit through the gate could walk right in, and they did, some hesitantly and some boldly. One day an exotic stranger arrived, pausing just for a moment to glance around cautiously, and then padding forward with confidence. He was a beautiful animal about the size of a small dog, golden red in color, with a fine brush of a tail, a sharp pointed muzzle, and piercing eyes.

The Hedge was something interesting in a dull landscape, and he was bored. He missed being chased all over the countryside by horsemen with red coats. But he couldn't help noticing that his arrival was causing a sensation, and not in a good way. The rabbits and the chickens especially ran away with screeches of alarm and hid behind trees. He could see them peering out and tried to reassure them. "You don't need to be afraid of me," he said, with a slightly injured air. "The White Mice taught us all much more civilized habits. Have you seen those lions and tigers outside enjoying their nice green salad for lunch? No, no, the old ways have changed. We can all be friends now."

This speech did little to reassure the animals, who followed him anxiously with their eyes as he arrived at the obvious cottage and entered Bistro Mole. There was a nervous flutter inside, and several sudden departures. Mole came out bravely from behind the counter and asked what the newcomer wanted.

"You must be the famous Mr. Mole," said the fox. "My name is Mr. Apex and I'm very pleased to meet you." Apex was an unusual name, but the fox's mother had heard somewhere that a fox was an apex predator, and she liked the sound of the word. Mr. Apex repeated to Mole the reassurances he had already given to the other animals, and asked if he could possibly get a dish of apples for his lunch.

"Plain or stewed apples?" asked Mole, still trembling a little.

"Oh, plain is fine, and how much do I owe you?"

"Owe me for what?" asked Mole, puzzled.

"For the apples, I have to pay for my food."

"No, you don't. Everything is free in Bistro Mole."

The fox was amazed, and rather upset. He had been a lawyer in the old Wide World, before people and money had vanished. The idea of anything being "free" had never entered his head, and he didn't like it. He remonstrated with the unhappy Mole and explained the principles of exchange and money.

"Now I understand," said Mole. "We had a wealthy Toad living here who was always talking about money, and getting it, and losing it. But we never used it ourselves, and now I suppose it doesn't exist anymore."

Mr. Apex was thoughtful. "I suppose you're right," he said reflectively. "But money was just pieces of paper or lines in a ledger. The main thing is to have *something* to exchange so that, for example, you Mr. Mole, as a businessman, can become rich.

Otherwise, there's no point to doing anything. Look," he said, grabbing a handful of fallen leaves from a nearby table, "Suppose this big oak leaf is a ten and this little Laurel leaf is a one, and all the other leaves have a value according to their name and size." He arranged four leaves in a line on the table. "You see. Oak is ten, apple is five, elm is two, and laurel is one – a total value of eighteen."

"Eighteen what?" asked the bewildered Mole.

"Eighteen anything, it doesn't matter. If you ask questions like that, you will never become rich," said the Fox severely. Mole thought that this whole conversation was completely nonsensical, but he agreed to introduce Mr. Apex to his more intellectual friends later that day.

"This is going to be a craze just like the clock," said Pegasus, gloomily, and he was absolutely right. The idea caught on at once, as all really silly ideas do. It was something new, and seemed somehow sophisticated. Mole reluctantly added prices to his menu at the bistro. At first, he priced everything at one leaf regardless of whether it was a bowl of water for a four-course vegetarian meal. The Fox explained that the price should correspond to the value of each item. But mole, the reluctant capitalist, argued that everything you really wanted had the same value at the moment you wanted it. A big meal had no value to someone who just wanted a drink of water. The Fox sighed.

But the animals in general were enchanted by their new economy. Leaves were easy to find, especially for the squirrels who pulled off whole branches and formed what they called a "Joint Stick Company." Everyone felt rather wealthy, and spent their time arranging and counting their leaves and trying to remember the totals. Even Water Rat began to charge a few leaves for pleasure trips on the river. Prices started to go up.

Badger and Pegasus were disgusted and refused to participate in the new leaf economy. They felt that the simple animals (and most of them were pretty simple), had been corrupted by the sly Fox. Toad had been a terrible example to them before, with his obsession with money, and now they were imitating him. But the more sensible animals could think of nothing to do about it.

However, as often happens, nature did something about it. Autumn was rapidly advancing and, although this meant more leaves on the ground at first, it soon became an economic disaster. About a billion leaves fell on their heads, and for a moment they were all immensely rich. Then massive inflation set in, and they were all wiped out. The usually cautious Bank Vole, who had invested as unwisely as anybody else, announced that nothing was worth anything, retired his security dormouse, and threw his accumulated leaves into the river. Even discounted pine needles found no takers. It was a trick that had been played a million times back in the old Wide World, often with money that did not even exist, even though humans claimed to have superior intelligence.

Apex the Fox left the community under a cloud. It was only when he was some distance away, gazing at the leafless landscape, that he realized that he himself was a victim of his own cleverness. He had accumulated a fortune in leaves. Now, he was broke.

Chapter nineteen: The Unseen University

Winter, with its leafless trees, chill winds and gray skies, was hard on the animals, but they made the best of it. Perhaps the luckiest were those who slept right through, but everyone else kept busy with domestic tasks and foraging for food in Mole's Bistro, and there were still weekly readings and tale tellings in the Obvious Cottage and the Castle, and the occasional musical evening at the Bistro.

On the musical side they had some limitations. They missed Slimena's strange and ethereal flute music and had to be content for the most part with the recordings available for the ancient wind-up phonograph. For accompaniment there was some syncopated drumming on biscuit tin lids, and some more or less tuneful squeaking, but it was not a sophisticated ensemble. Some of the rats were experimenting with the cello that had been found in the junk room. They laid it flat on the ground while two rats handled the fingering at the top and two more scraped the bow back and forth, one holding each end. It was a severe handicap that they had no readable music, but some of the effects they produced were undoubtedly original. They specialized in operatic arias they had learned by heart from the phonograph records. Anyone who has not heard grand opera as interpreted by four rats on a horizontal cello has a remarkable musical experience still in store.

What flourished especially this winter was the Unseen University, so-called because it was so difficult to find. It occupied some dark, warm rooms in a remote corner of the Obvious Cottage and had been established largely by accident the year before by the newly-arrived tortoise, Tardy, who had been a teacher in his previous life. There was only one student at first, Dozy the Dormouse who found the Professor's droning voice pleasantly soporific. But the word spread, the student body doubled to two, and then more, and soon a motley crowd of animals came every day – some to sleep and some to hear the learned tortoise, who now styled himself Herr Doctor Professor Doctor Tardy. After a while he also appointed himself Chancellor, President, Dean of Animals, Head of Department and (just in case) Professor Emeritus. There were no tuition fees because, in effect, there was no tuition. Admission was open to anyone who could find the right room, and many animals never did. But an hour spent with the professor was just about the best winter entertainment that the Wild Wood could provide.

Professor Tardy was often late to class, having got lost on the way to the University, and was routinely rescued by the Messenger Mice. For this reason, and for his habit of going to sleep during classes, he was affectionately known as the invisible professor of the Unseen University. He presided over a nonexistent faculty consisting entirely of his own graduates, for reasons that will be explained later if any explanation proves possible.

There was no curriculum to speak of, so nobody spoke of it. But when Professor Tardy was there, and awake, he would pose tricky questions such as: "Is

Water Rat's hedge a symbol, a metaphor, a metonym, a synonym, a palindrome, or just a nice piece of topiary?" or "Are we all fiction, and how would we know?" or "What is the point of rabbits?" He had borrowed this last especially challenging question from the Medical Bear. It has puzzled philosophers down the ages, and found no sensible answers here.

All these questions were discussed in great detail, and at the end of the session, students were encouraged to write their answers on a postcard and place them in a box in front of the desk, where Prof. Tardy was dozing. The box was never emptied.

Sometimes the Professor would introduce regular school subjects in the hope of making his students more educated in the old-world sense. For example: "There are five branches of arithmetic: the first four are ambition, distraction, amplification, and derision. What is the fifth branch and why?" On one memorable occasion he even ventured on literature and announced that he was about to read the work of a very famous author, Marcel Proust. This caused to great anxiety to Pegasus who was attending the University extension – just outside the window – and knew from his past experience of listening to books that the works of this particular author were immensely long and almost impossible to understand, or even to survive. But he need not have worried. What Prof. Tardy had found was merely a page torn from the book from which he read the following sentence in his scratchy voice.

"But when from a long distant past nothing subsists, after the people are dead, after the things are broken and scattered, taste and smell alone, more fragile but more enduring, more immaterial, more persistent, more faithful, remain poised for a long time, like souls, remembering, waiting, hoping, and amidst the ruins of all the rest; and bear unflinchingly in the tiny and almost impalpable drop of their essence, the vast structure of recollection."

There was a long pause in which a small voice could be heard asking: "Is it lunchtime yet?" The professor waited in vain for a further response from his students, and then dropped the page into the waste basket, and moved on to a reading from Edward Lear about an owl and a pussycat, which the class would have found much more interesting if any of them had still been awake.

The somewhat eclectic nature of classes at the unseen University had a lot to do with the professor's methods of research. He borrowed material from Badger's library which now included charred fragments of books from what had been the much larger library at Toad Hall, spread them out on the floor and crept about reading them more or less at random. Like Badger himself he had no way of distinguishing fact from fiction or sense from nonsense. It all seemed like good teaching material. It was perhaps unfortunate that one of the more complete books he had found was a set of stories by a man called the Rev. Dodgson that contained a great many strange animals and a great deal of eccentric philosophy, all of which seemed perfectly sound to Professor Tardy. So, the class often spent valuable educational time discussing walruses and carpenters, snarks, white rabbits, and Cheshire cats, enjoying every minute of it but not making much intellectual progress. Fortunately, in this new world intellectual progress was completely useless. As Pegasus constantly pointed out, all that an animal ever needed was common sense and a sense of fun. Proust had nothing useful to say to the creatures of the Wild Wood.

None of this mattered in any case because everyone graduated with an A. The UU grading system had been worked out by one of the Lab rats who considered himself a statistician. It was based on the principle that every student who failed to get an A must inevitably get an F because the intermediate grades were just too confusing. Credit was given for class participation and for keeping quiet or sleeping so that others could participate. This system guaranteed that every student would get an A, and graduate with honors. Higher degrees were awarded impartially on the basis of attendance or non-attendance, so everybody got one and immediately joined the faculty. Very soon there were more faculty than students, which suited everybody because students are nothing but a nuisance.

Some animals from the outside spoke ironically about the Unseen University with its Invisible Professor, Imaginary Faculty, and Nonexistent Students. But Professor Tardy had lived long in the Old World, and he knew that imaginary institutions are beyond the reach of irony. The trouble comes when someone starts pretending that they are real.

After a while Badger, Pegasus and other members of what they secretly called the 'sensible party' became reconciled to the Unseen University. The young animals enjoyed it and learned how to talk and argue, and even occasionally to think. They also learned a lot of new words, because the Professor really was a very learned tortoise. It was, they all agreed at last, a credit to the community, whatever those envious zoo animals might say.

Chapter twenty: The Return of Toad (again)

Winter that year was chill and windy, but not cold enough to freeze the river or provide snow, so there was no winter festival like last year's. The animals were looking for a diversion, and it came one frosty morning when the rabbits, playing by the river, heard the strangest sound. It was a high, wavering, almost unearthly note that went on and on, seeming to come from somewhere downstream. The senior rabbit, Mr. Bunnyface (who was more mature than most of the rabbits, but not by much) pricked up his large ears and listened hard.

"I can't be sure," he said, in a wondering voice, "But it sounds like Slimena's flute music. How can she be here?"

The next thing was, if possible, even more surprising. As they gazed down the river two huge gray monsters with UPS painted on their sides came into view, plodding sedately along the towpath one behind the other and linked by a length of rope. Behind them another length of rope stretched out until a boat could be seen through the morning haze. They were pulling it along like a barge, and the rabbits recognized it as Toad's little steam boat, dirty and battered with its funnel leaning to one side, but still afloat.

The excitement was enormous. The rabbits rushed off to spread the news, then rushed back so as not to miss anything, then rushed off again because they had forgotten to spread the news the first time. Messenger mice were dispatched, but their information was so confusing that the whole community soon gathered by the river to see what was really happening. Meanwhile the huge gray monsters arrived and, seeing the crowd, stopped and waved their trunks in a friendly fashion.

"Good morning," said the first, "Chilly for the time of year. Is this the neighborhood known as The Riverbank?" They said it was. "We have a delivery for you, or rather two deliveries. We don't know exactly what they are but one of them is in a bad way, and the other plays the flute all the time. They are both very ugly. Can we leave them with you?"

Slimena came out of the little cabin and stood on the deck, surveying the crowd of amazed animals.

"We are back," she announced, grandly. "These two ladies," she gestured with her flute at the monsters,

"Have saved us from a terrible fate and brought us home. But His Majesty back there is a bit upset by it all, so perhaps we can take him to the Castle and let him rest."

So, yet again, Toad arrived home as an invalid, or at least as a nervous wreck. He kept babbling about Monsters, so the Medical Bear was called. This threw Toad into a panic, although the Medical Bear was the friendliest bear that you could possibly imagine, and not at all big and intimidating like some of his relatives. The Bear observed the hysterical Toad for a while through a keyhole and decided that there was not much physically wrong with him.

"He seems to be suffering from what we call PTSD or Paranoid Toad Stress Disorder," the bear diagnosed. "He has developed an irrational fear of what he calls Monsters, which means just about all the animals in the outside world, especially the big ones, and even me. All I can suggest is rest and quiet and familiar company for a while, and you may have your old Toad back again." (Although why you should want him back I can't imagine, the Bear added to himself.)

So Toad was installed in a quiet room of the Castle, and his friends came one by one to sit with him until he was restored to whatever kind of sanity he was capable of. At first, he raved about having a watchtower built on top of the Castle to watch for Monsters, and guards to defend against them. But he was assured by Badger that this would be a waste of time because Monsters were already everywhere. Regular paths now led from the Zoo Lake to the Castle and the Bridge, and animals of all sizes walked freely in all directions. Toad did not want to hear this but was eventually persuaded to look for himself and see that it was true.

After a couple of weeks of being calmed and pampered he was more like himself, which was no great improvement. But he felt that he had to tell his story because, on the face of things, the whole episode had been horribly embarrassing. Toad had set off with great fanfare to discover a new world and had come back without apparently discovering anything and in a state of collapse. What happened? The animals were dying to know. So, a meeting was set up in Toad's room with just a small private group: Slimena, Water Rat, Mole, Badger, and of course Emelia Ermine to take notes. Toad promised to tell them everything, but Slimena was determined to tell the whole truth and nothing but the truth, which was a very different matter. So their story went like this.

Toad: We sailed boldly down the river past the hedge and out to sea like fearless explorers. Nothing could stop us.

Slimena: Actually you ran into the river bank three times, and nearly blew up the boiler by putting on too much fuel. Whenever we saw a big animal, you hid in the cabin.

Toad: When we reached the sea it was terrifying, the waves were mountainous, much higher than the funnel. We couldn't possibly survive, but we pressed on regardless, willing to sacrifice anything to reach our goal.

Slimena: It was as calm as a mill pond, but you began feeling sick as soon as you realized that we had left the river and were out at sea.

Toad: We sailed across the vast ocean for what seemed like days and days without any sight of land until we ran out of wood for fuel and ran out of food. We had no sails or oars, so we were becalmed out there with no chance of ever being rescued.

Slimena: The boat kept going for about half an hour before the fuel ran out, but we could see land on all sides. We still had plenty of food, but Toad was too sick to eat it.

The attentive reader of this saga will realize instantly what had happened here (as Water Rat did, but he was too polite to interrupt). Toad had sailed his little steamer out into Hopewell Bay, the same bay where Water Rat had been lost on his great sailing adventure. Toad's expedition was not anywhere near the open ocean let alone close to finding the new motoring paradise that he had been dreaming of. But the account went on in much the same back-and-forth way, and the animals watched it like fascinated spectators at a tennis match.

Toad: Suddenly we were surrounded by vast whales that threatened to devour us along with the boat.

Slimena: We met some nice seals who asked if we were in trouble and whether they could help. Toad was hiding in the cabin again screaming about being eaten by a herd of whales.

Toad: We were doomed, and then suddenly we found ourselves safely at the shore, tied up by a little jetty, and Slimena was having tea with the whales. I must say she was very brave.

Slimena: The seals were wonderful. They pushed the boat to a place on shore where we could tie it up, and they stayed for tea. There are lots of animals around here who belonged to a circus in the old days. It was probably the same circus that turned Toad into a clown. (Toad groaned). We were going to camp there for a while, but it was freezing and too cramped in the cabin. So, the seals found us those two beautiful elephants. Both of them had been called jumbo in the circus but really they are Sarah and Eloise, and they have set up a delivery business called UPS, or

Universal Pachyderm Service. Their motto is: "A slow delivery is a safe delivery" and they have been very successful with people who are not in a hurry. They agreed to tow us, with the little steamboat, back up the river to the Castle, and here we are."

Toad had nothing to say about this, other than some mutterings about not trusting the big gray monsters. They had stayed on for a while, having no new deliveries to make, and told their story about life in the circus, and how they had been made to do ridiculous and undignified tricks. They remembered Toad's appearance in the ring as a clown and declared that he had been funnier than any clown they had ever seen. Toad turned his back and pretended not to hear this..

The elephants asked polite questions about the neighborhood, and the mysterious Hedge that surrounded it, and they were especially interested to hear about the former zoo not far away and the many exotic animals that continued to live in that area, including some elephants. An expedition was proposed, and soon Sarah and Eloise set off on the path to the zoo lake with Water Rat riding precariously on top of Sarah as a guide. Toad retired to his room in the Castle and sullenly watched them go. These huge animals offended his sense of proportion, in which Toad himself was always supposed to be the biggest and bravest thing around.

The future looked very boring. He needed a new idea, a new project, and new adventure - one that preferably did not involve boats or monsters. He began to think, trying to ignore the ethereal sound of Slimena's flute. Was there inspiration to be found in music? He very much doubted it and buried his head under a pillow.

Winter crept by in a haze of sleepiness and indolence as usual. Most animals did nothing, or less than nothing, but the ladies of Slimena's salon had been busy.

One early spring morning Toad was about to settle in his usual place by the window, where he would spend the day gazing out at the dull, car-free landscape. Something was blocking his view, a large jar full of murky water with live things wriggling in it. Toad jumped back.

"What's this horrible thing?" he yelled. Slimena was standing just behind him, waiting to see his reaction.

"That, my dear Toad, is your future," she said sweetly, or as sweetly as she could. "There have always been Toads here on the Riverbank, I saw your family tree in Toad Hall. Now the Toad Dynasty will continue forever, and the responsibility is all yours."

Toad gazed at the toadpoles with loathing and buried his head in his hands.

Chapter twenty-one – Dynasty

All the animals loved to play outdoors in the summer although their antics, which usually involved wild chases and plunges into the river, rather pained Mr. Badger. He thought that they were rather disorganized, not to say chaotic, and that they would benefit from a bit of discipline and a set of rules. But what rules he could not say. Rules of any kind were not much used or understood in the Willows community, and discipline was unknown.

The inhabitants of the old world, as far as he could learn from the scraps of literature and memorabilia that he had collected, were passionately attached to what they called sports. These seemed to be highly organized forms of childish play. But the only information Badger possessed was a few ancient photographs and confusing descriptions like "Bottom of the ninth" or "field goal." Almost all the games involved a ball of some kind, big or small. In some pictures it was being carried about a field, in others it was kicked, or hit with a stick, and in yet others thrown in the air. The point of all these activities was completely mysterious, although Toad's humiliating experiment with golf suggested that numbers had something to do with it.

Pegasus was helpful here, as he so often was, having spent so much time in the Wide World and being an observant horse. He had names for most of the "sports" – football, cricket, tennis, and so on – and some general idea of how they were played. But the big problem, he pointed out, was that most of their four-footed friends were unable to play the old human games. They couldn't kick, carry, or hit the ball with their paws, although squirrels showed some skill at throwing acorns.

"It's unnatural," said Pegasus. "Animals already have their own games, and we don't need to encourage them to make teams and have competitions. That was the whole downfall of the human world."

An entirely different kind of recreation was needed. They all thought about it but failed to come up with anything more original than running wildly around in circles or, in the case of squirrels, up and down, which the animals did very well already. Quizzes, cards, and indoor games had no appeal, especially not in summer.

Professor Tardy offered one or two suggestions from his collection of peculiar books. One was an activity called croquet, which seemed to require nothing more than some small hedgehogs and a few flamingoes. The young hedgehogs were willing to roll about in the grass, but when Magpie went to see the handsome pink flamingoes who lived on the zoo lake, he got a flat refusal.

"We know all about that," they squawked indignantly. "People were always shouting "Croquet, croquet" at us when we were in the zoo, and we've read the book (or at least that part of it). Croquet mallets, phooey!"

So that was the end of croquet, and the Professor's only other suggestion was a rather complicated game called chess which required no ball and involved no running about at all. They gave it a try, marking out sixty-four rather uneven squares on a flat piece of the Riverbank and assigning animals to their positions. The rabbits and squirrels were pawns opposite sides, the hedgehogs were castles because they lived in one, the frogs were knights because they hopped about, and so on. The kings and queens were a problem. Toad and Slimena flatly refused to play, even if they could wear crowns, and Badger had to approach the farm animals who volunteered a hen and a rooster and two more or less indistinguishable white ducks.

Badger read out the rules in a booming, hieratic voice. This took about half an hour, by which time the orderly chess board had become a confused mass of very confused animals, many of them asleep. Badger finally announced: "Rabbits move first," at which signal they all abandoned the game and rushed off to Bistro Mole. So that was the end of chess.

The older and more sedate members of the community (although "sedate" is putting it a bit strong) were disinclined to join in these shenanigans, either because of their sedateness, or because they were old, tired, overweight, or just plain lazy. For these solid citizens the clubs provided a place of refuge and source of companionship and entertainment. The oldest club, in the Obvious Cottage (and therefore now called the Obvious Club) was the most popular because it was closest to Mole's Bistro. But all the others had loyal members.

The Amphibian's Club had moved. It had been temporarily housed on the old barge moored outside the ruins of Toad Hall, but the barge had drifted away once and now was slowly sinking. Some members thought this was fine, but others complained that it was rapidly becoming the Underwater Club. Toad roused himself and negotiated a deal with Ms Tiggywinkle in the Old Castle, where there was plenty of space. The Castle, like the Obvious Cottage, had an apparently infinite number of rooms, and the Amphibian's Club was re-established on the ground floor. This was ideal because the Beavers, with their constant dam-building activity, flooded the floor at least once a week. This made the Amphibians feel comfortably at home, and the club flourished.

The Frequent Flyers Club also flourished and became even more decorative because of the arrival of exotic birds from the former zoo. The birds, of course, recognized no frontiers, not even Water Rat's Hedge. So, their meetings now included a great many talkative parrots in a rainbow of colors, as well as hornbills, peafowl, and even some puffins.

Slimena's Salon, which had been displaced from the Hall when Toad burned it down, was also re-established in one of the towers of the castle. It attracted an enthusiastic group of female animals who, however, had little in common. This did not prevent them from talking incessantly, and Slimena was too lazy to use her position as ChairToad to impose any kind of order. It was the Orakitten, now fully grown and known deferentially as Oracula, who brought forward an idea that got some of them excited. She had a reputation for wisdom and even for mysterious magical powers that had rubbed off from her association with the Oracat. Now she decided to use it.

"We shall have a séance," she announced one day, and then had to spend a lot of time explaining what a séance was, and what fun it would be to call up their animal ancestors, and perhaps learn some spicy secrets from the past. Not all the ladies thought that this was a good idea. Some of them had spicy secrets of their own. But they agreed to sit in a circle in a darkened room (darkened as much in the holes in the wall would permit) and hold hands.

Oracula took the chair as the Medium, and tried to contact some of her own ancestors. But the spirit would was more complicated than she thought. Cats have at least nine lives, and the resulting hordes of undead` cats, all unhappy about being woken up, created spiritual chaos.

In the midst of this strangeness, something even stranger happened. A puff of pink smoke erupted in the middle of the table, making them all jump back. When the smoke cleared they saw a White Mouse, waving her paws furiously.

"No, no, no, no," she was saying. "Stop this at once. We went to a lot of trouble to give you a sensible new world to live in. We wiped out thousands of religions, cults, illusions, superstitions, and lunatic beliefs, and here you are trying to start it all up again. This world should be enough of a miracle for you."

The ladies of the club were all ashamed of themselves, especially Oracula, and the mouse spoke more kindly. She was, they learned, not the original Spokesmouse Ethel, but a Troubleshooting mouse by the name of Fiona. Her job was to roam the galaxy in search of wickedness or religion (which the mice assumed were much the same) and put the guilty creatures back on track.

"Think about this," she said. "What is the future of this lovely community? I don't see many young animals around. What about that remarkable Mr. Toad of yours. Who will cause chaos and excitement when he's gone?" And the mouse fixed her pink eyes on Slimena, who shrank back in her seat.

"Think of the future, ladies. Consider who will populate this wonderful community of yours when you are gone. Do your duty." Fiona looked at them all, in turn, and added: "Don't run away with the idea that we white mice are some kind of God's, or spirits, or angels or all-powerful beings from another galaxy. We are just white mice, and mice advice is good advice." She vanished in a puff of pink smoke, only to return a second later to add: "And the pink smoke is just a special effect." And she vanished again leaving the members of Slimena's salon staring at the pink smoke drifting over the empty table stunned, disturbed, but rather excited.

Winter drifted by in a haze of sleepiness and indolence as usual. Most animals did nothing, or less than nothing, but the ladies of Slimena's salon had been busy.

One early spring morning Toad was about to settle in his usual place by the window, where he would spend the day gazing out at the dull, car-free landscape. Something was blocking his view, a large jar full of murky water with live things wriggling in it. Toad jumped back.

"What's this horrible thing?" he yelled. Slimena was standing just behind him, waiting to see his reaction.

"That, my dear Toad, is your future," she said sweetly, or as sweetly as she could. "There have always been Toads here on the Riverbank, I saw your family tree in Toad Hall. Now the Toad Dynasty will continue forever, and the responsibility is all yours."

Toad gazed at the toadpoles with loathing and buried his head in his hands.

Chapter twenty-two – New World Symphony

The appearance of the Toadpoles set off a silent battle between Toad and Slimena. Every morning Toad would remove the jar from his sunny window and put it in a dark corner of the room. A few minutes later Slimena would put it back on the windowsill again.

"This is your heritage," she would tell him, "This is your future." Other ladies from Slimena's salon came in from time to time and repeat the same message to an unresponsive toad who continued to regard the Toadpoles with disgust. As the months went by they grew, without becoming any more beautiful. But they also changed, becoming more and more like miniature versions of Toad himself. One day, instead of bringing the jar back to the window, Slimena showed him a tray with half a dozen little Toadlet's hopping around on it. "You had better wake up Toad," she told him. "One of these little chaps is going to be taking your place one of these days. It's time you started paying attention to his upbringing.

This idea shocked toad extremely. He had never thought about being replaced. After all he was the Great Toad, the biggest and most colorful personality on the Riverbank. How could one of these vile little Toadlets possibly replace him? But it was undeniable that they looked rather like him, one in particular slightly larger than the rest, with a cheeky face and a lively way of hopping about and banging into things that seemed strangely familiar to Toad. But Toad had no idea about bringing up any of these youngsters. He had never been brought up himself, but just watched what his father did and imitated that. Slimena, of course, had plenty of ideas.

Thus began a long process, at first very tedious but later more interesting for Toad and Slimena, of educating the Toadlets for their future positions in Riverbank society. Toad made no secret of his preference for the biggest and liveliest Toadlet who he named Hercules. Young Hercule was a handful from the start, but a quick learner. He remembered the names of all Toad's wrecked cars but, more surprisingly, he was equally quick to recognize and name the plants and birds. Toad was tormented by the thought that he might have produced a naturalist or, worse, an unnatural toad.

There were great changes along the Riverbank and in the Wildwood that spring. Many more animals appeared. The rabbits had multiplied as always, and the squirrels too. But small creatures of every kind could be seen and often tripped over everywhere. Even the birds had nests full of birdlings and were laboriously training them to fly. Not everyone was sure where these offspring came from, or why, or how. They tended to blame the white mice. The Orakitten produced half a dozen charming Orakitten kittens in different colors, to the absolute horror of the Oracat, Water Rat and Mole were both being followed about by tiny versions of themselves and even Badger with great embarrassment admitted to a family connection with an adorable young badger kitt that he claimed he was looking after for someone else.

The antics of all these youngsters, and their frequent need to be rescued from thoughtless scrapes, helped to fill the gap left by the far less active Toad. He had entertained the whole community with one disaster after another but, after his recent violent adventures, he was more tired than he wanted to admit. The community secretly hoped that Young Hercule (who had a wicked gleam in his glaucous eye) would prove to be just as amusing, although perhaps less destructive. Hercule had an equally lively sister, Helena, and who knew what she might be capable of when Toad had completed her education?

The medical Bear was kept busy tending to all these new arrivals. He padded from burrow to burrow, tree to tree, and nest to nest, patiently and good humoredly checking out all the little animals and birds with his stethoscope and pronouncing them wonderfully healthy. Indeed there was nothing to make them sick, apart from overeating. The Medical Bear's well-meaning efforts to introduce a diet and exercise regime were met with a universal "Phooey." But it was the Medical Bear who first raised a doubt about Hercules, whispering something in Slimena's ear here during one of his regular visits to the castle. Slimena went very pale but said nothing to Toad for the moment. This was a problem that had to be dealt with very carefully, but not a problem that entirely displeased her.

For news of the outside world, the community relied on Pegasus and the Old Goat. These two companions, who loved the open road, wandered far and wide over the new landscape and brought back reports. These, edited and improved by Sally Stoat and Emilia Ermine, provided the basis for a series of travel articles called "Around The New World" in the *Riverbank Record.* Sometimes the travelers would take Water Rat with them, to render the scenes they saw into art, and even into poetry. One of his poems about daffodils was particularly admired.

What they saw was indeed astonishing, even to such sophisticated animals. Untold millions of trees that had once been cut down by men for fuel, or to clear land, or to build machines of war had grown again, so that vast forests covered the land. There were grasslands and meadows, full of plants long ago wiped out by the human habit of spraying poisons, that stretched away into the hills. All the extinct plants and vegetables had come back, and their flowers and blossoms made a blaze of colors. The rivers were clear and pure, and there was such an abundance of food and space that the animals could live in harmony with no more than the usual small arguments over nesting sites and inter-species banter. It was a true Eden in which even the snakes could find nobody worth tempting. The weather, of course, was perfect, with no more than the occasional white cloud and exactly the right amount of rain. The white mice were very pleased with it. "Second time lucky," they squeaked with satisfaction.

Back on the Riverbank an important real estate deal was concluded at the Old Castle. Ms Tiggywinkle was ready to retire as *Chateleine.* She was quite worn out by cleaning up after the Beavers and wanted a quiet life while still staying in the social center of things. So, she retired back to her old quarters in the West Tower, and Toad and Slimena delightedly took charge of the rest, renaming the ancient fortress Castle Toad. The Beavers remained in residence, but at least half the castle stayed dry and the wet half made an appropriate new home for the Amphibian Club.

The only cloud on the horizon was Toad's favorite Toadlet, his presumed heir and successor. When they moved into new quarters in the castle Young Hercule showed an inexplicable interest in home decorating, and quite good taste. He spent more time in Badger's library than with Toad's collection of wrecked cars, and even expressed an interest in poetry that Water Rat was pleased to encourage. Toad became very worried.

Slimena, encouraged by the ladies of her salon, decided that she could not wait any longer. The blow fell as Toad was instructing young Hercules in the intricacies of speed limits, police traps, and the procedure in magistrate's courts.

"Toad," she said carefully, "This is not the kind of thing that a nice young lady toad needs to know." It took Toad a while to understand this, but eventually he did.

"You mean he's a girl!" he screamed. All the dreams of a Toad dynasty that he had been building up collapsed. At first he looked hopefully at young Helena, but it turned out that she was a girl too!

So, in the most unexpected and delightful way, Castle Toad became a matriarchy. The Old Toad regime of chaos was slowly replaced by a civilized and even cultured community, in which car chases were never even mentioned. Toad admitted defeat, although not gracefully. There was a nonviolent handover of power, after which he spent much of his time reading his own exciting memoirs and sitting in the old garage communing with his collection of wrecked cars.

It was as peaceful as could be. Ms Tiggywinkle, knitting comfortably by the fire surrounded by yet another squad of Grand-Hoglets, with Dennis the Dragon sleeping in the ashes, watched it all with quiet satisfaction. A group of young Beavers rushed through the living room, carrying wood and dripping water all over the floor.

"It's just as I always told them," she said to herself. "It's all repetition." And for the third time that afternoon, she fell asleep.

THE END

Printed in Dunstable, United Kingdom